A Moment With...

"Inspirational writings and photographs to capture life's most touching moments"

Dr. Julianne Freiwald - Gaule

A Moment With...

ISBN: 978-1-970153-11-8
Library of Congress Control Number: 2020900416

Photo Credits

Cover - SUNSET Sky photograph by John Grundy

Interior Photo Photographers

John Grundy
Catherine Orban
David Gaule
Getty I-Stock Images

La Maison Publishing, Inc.
Vero Beach, Florida
The Hibiscus City

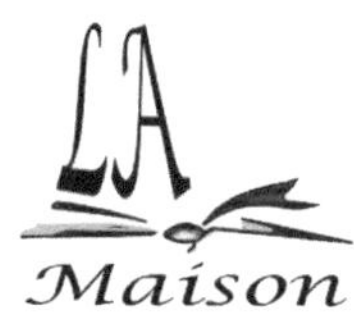

I dedicate this scenic and inspirational book to readers who are inspired by nature.

A special thanks to my parents and my late grandmother who fostered my writings since early childhood.

Also, my loving husband David Gaule.

Butterflies: A Moment with...

Transformation into a butterfly
takes a period of metamorphosis.
Our relationships change
by the way of life's forces.

A butterfly's life span
ranges from one month to nine.
Our gestation in utero
is the same frame of time.

A butterfly has plants
and gardens for its needs.
Our food and shelter exist
in communities.

We are like butterflies
as we stretch our own wings,
as we flutter through life's garden
with such beautiful things.

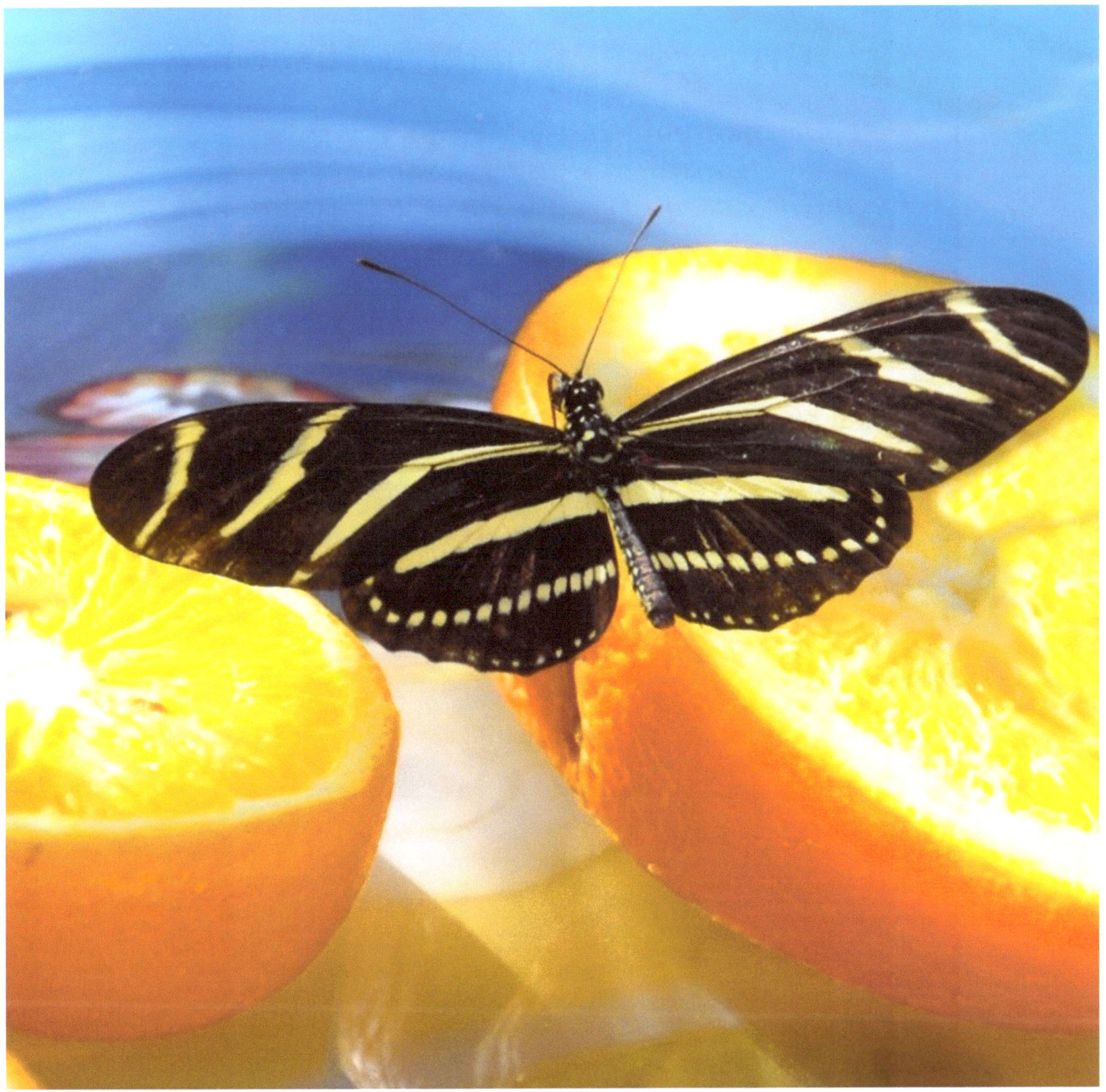

Giving: A Moment with...

When you find your inner gift,
you'll want to share it with others,
for in the act of giving is the art of receiving.

From the soul of one's heart is where giving is made.
Nothing in return should reflect what is laid.

The spirit of giving is from what's been created.
No one should view it as receiving until satiated.

This is why we know that giving is real.
One must feel it without expectations
or an exchange to heal.

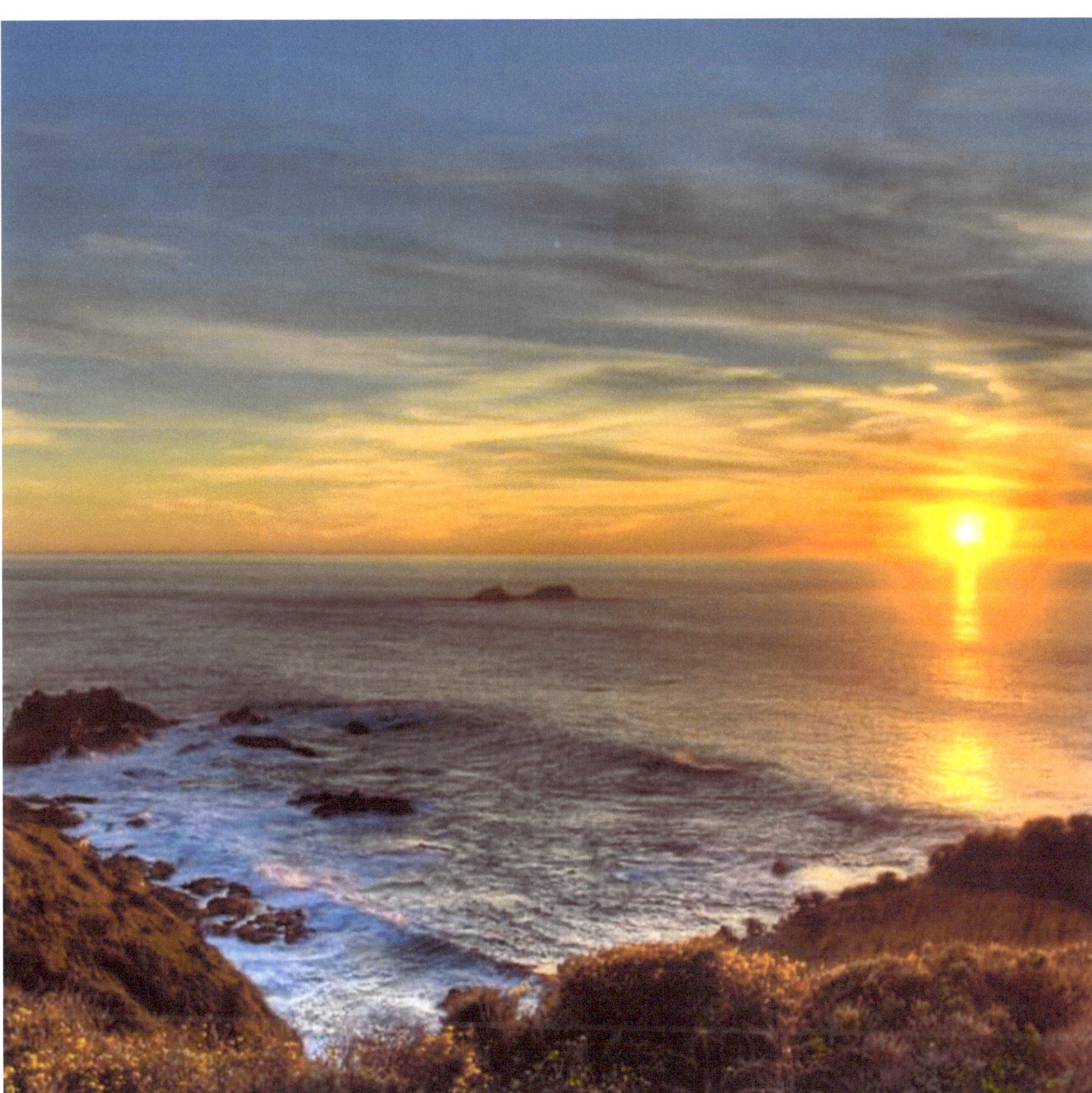

Whimsical Garden: A Moment with…

While stepping along a shaded path within a fanciful garden,
a fallen tree creates a seat
for those to rest their weary feet.

Birds are chirping in nests nearby
announcing the crack of dawn.
Blissful colors paint the lawn
while one can gaze at a timid fawn.

Glistening lily pads float across effervescent ponds.
Sparkling dewdrops tempt the fairies
lighting their way with wands.

Baby frogs take pleasure as
their playground becomes alive.
They leap across little brown logs
while scouting nearby flies.

The shadows and the breeze reflect the tadpoles squirming.
The snapping turtles raise their heads
to compete in water churning.

Cascading waterfalls heard from afar
blend with natures timing.
The wind blows through various trees
and forever we hear what's chiming.

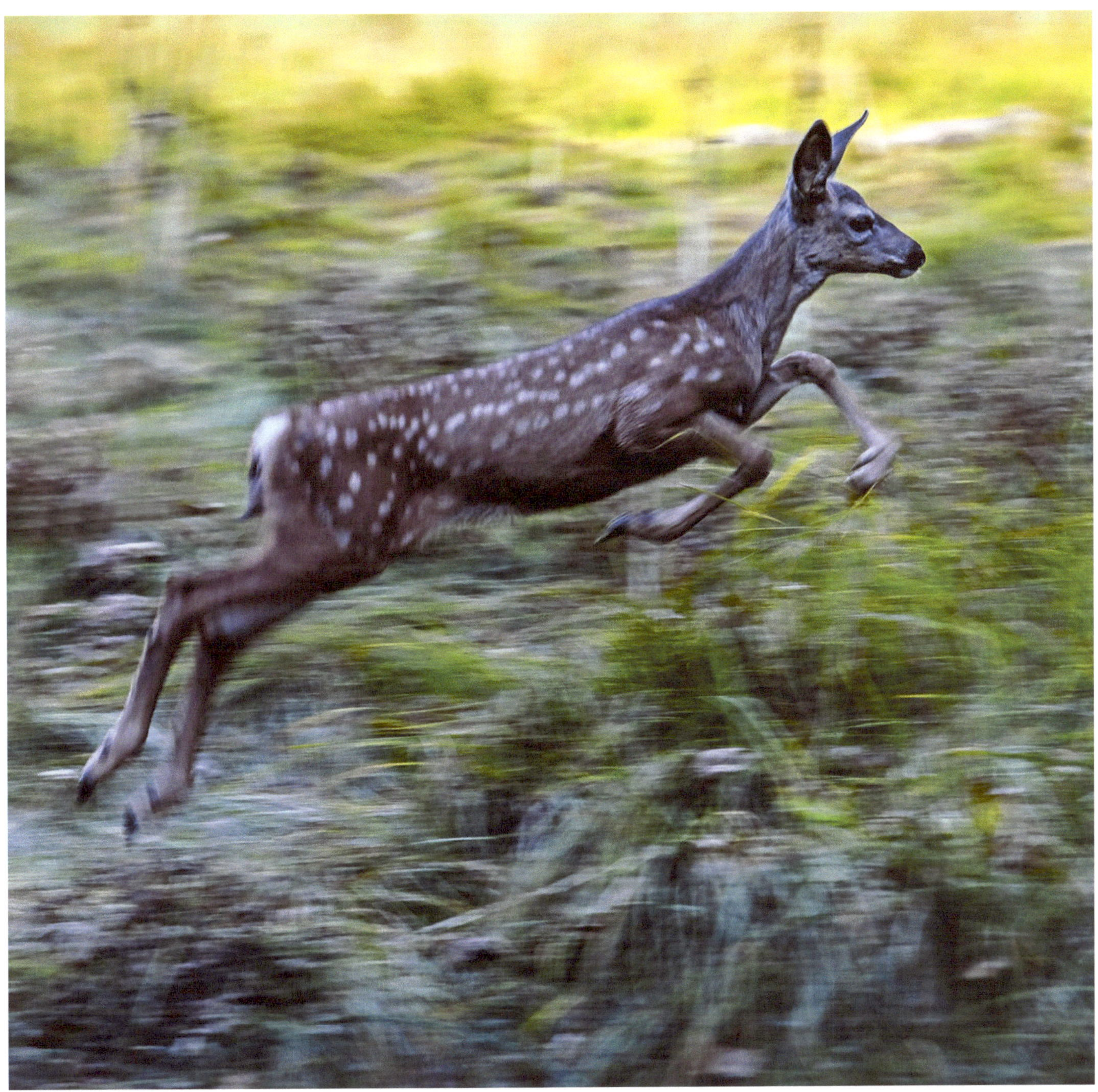

Doors of Life: A Moment with...

Doors open and close throughout one's life.
Trust the unique timing and pass through the light.

As one door shuts, others will open,
while creating a new bridge with no words spoken.
Forgive yourself and others too,
then acceptance is all you need to walk through.

One day it happens and you reflect on the construction.
Your life unfolded without destruction.

Be thankful for trusting intuition over ration,
For you'll discover a gift and new passion.

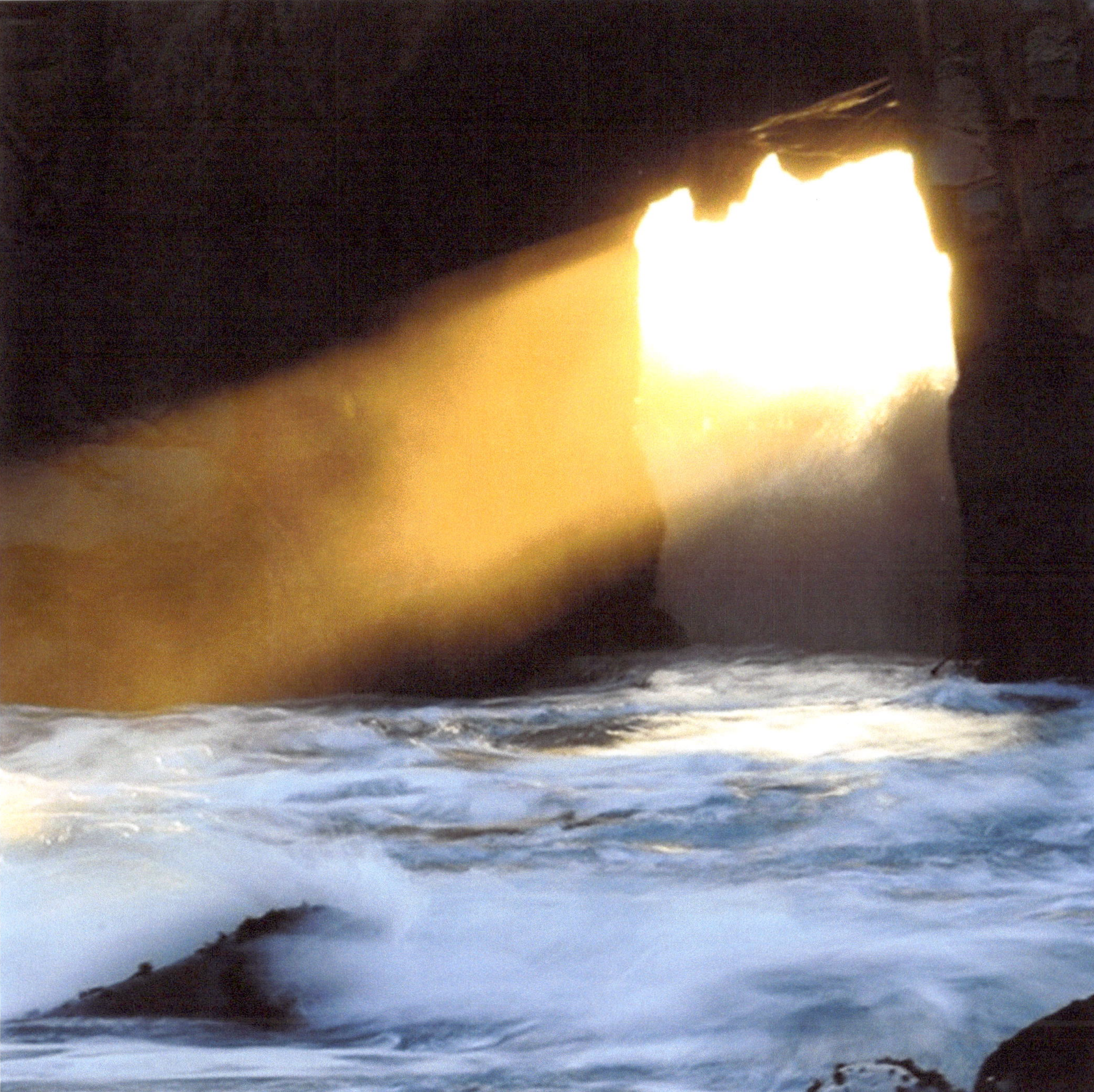

Ireland: A Moment with...

Ireland is a place of beauty
beyond what words can express.
It is mystical in nature
and a country that is blessed.

The Emerald Isle of rolling hills,
see the castles and the old cathedrals.
Walk the streets on the old cobblestones,
then sit and eat the Irish scones.

God put a piece of heaven right among the seas.
From north to south and east to west,
the people seem so pleased.

The Cliffs of Moher and the misty seas
are a lasting gift to all mankind.
The sheep that roam the Ring of Kerry,
the golden bushes are divine.

The colorful doors and the old thatched roofs
are inviting you to stay.
The natural wonders on an isle of grace,
call out for you to embrace.

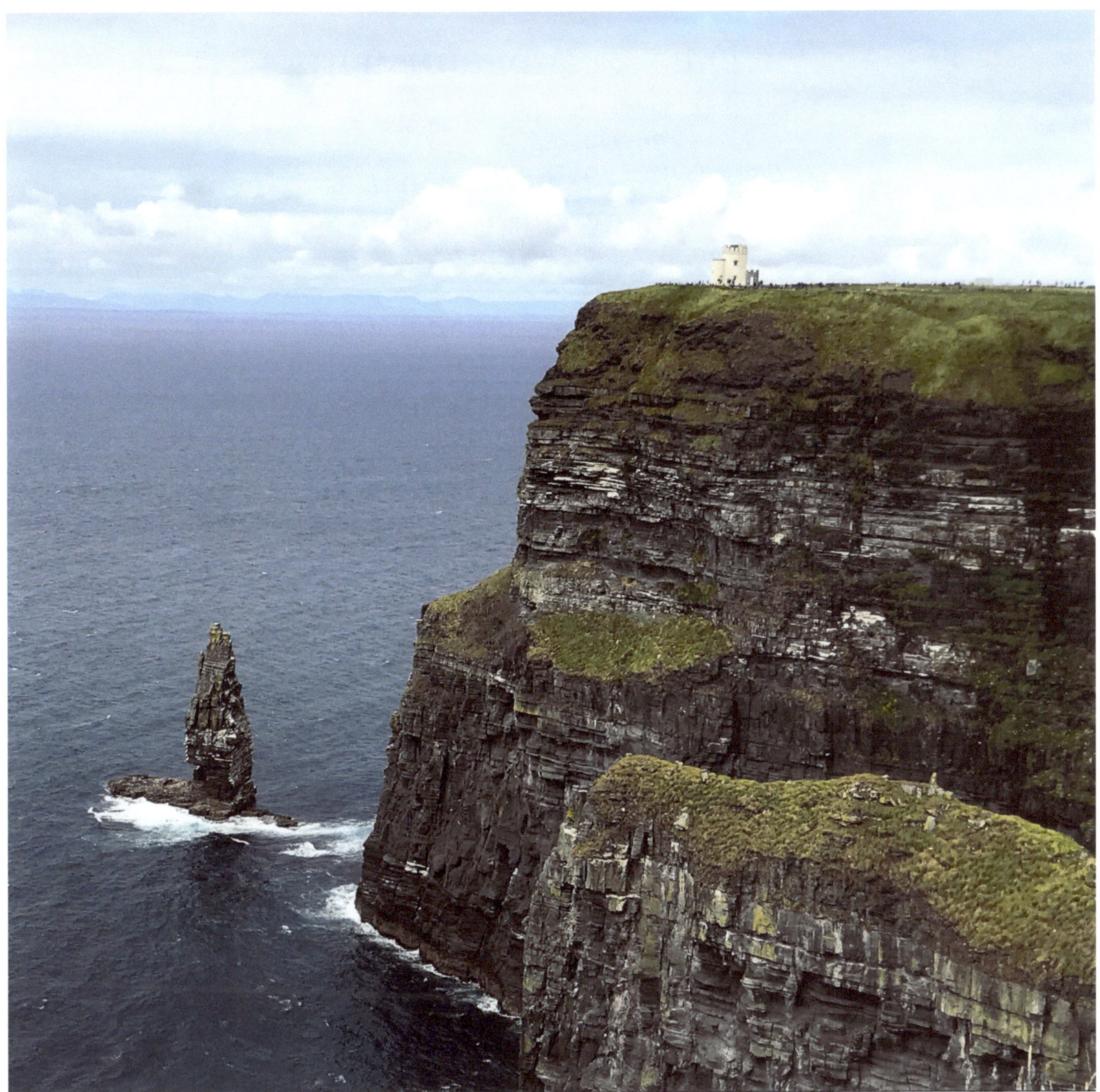

Patience: A Moment with...

Patience is one
of the gifts of the spirit.
It is present to those
who wait to experience it.

Endurance tests our patience
so we will not flee,
yet fortitude pays off
as you will soon see.

Timing is never
how long you anticipate,
but patience is always
worth its wait.

Step out of the way
of anxiety and fear,
instead be hopeful
as patience grows near.

Actions put forward
will help the time pass,
like waiting for a bloom
from a wild cactus.

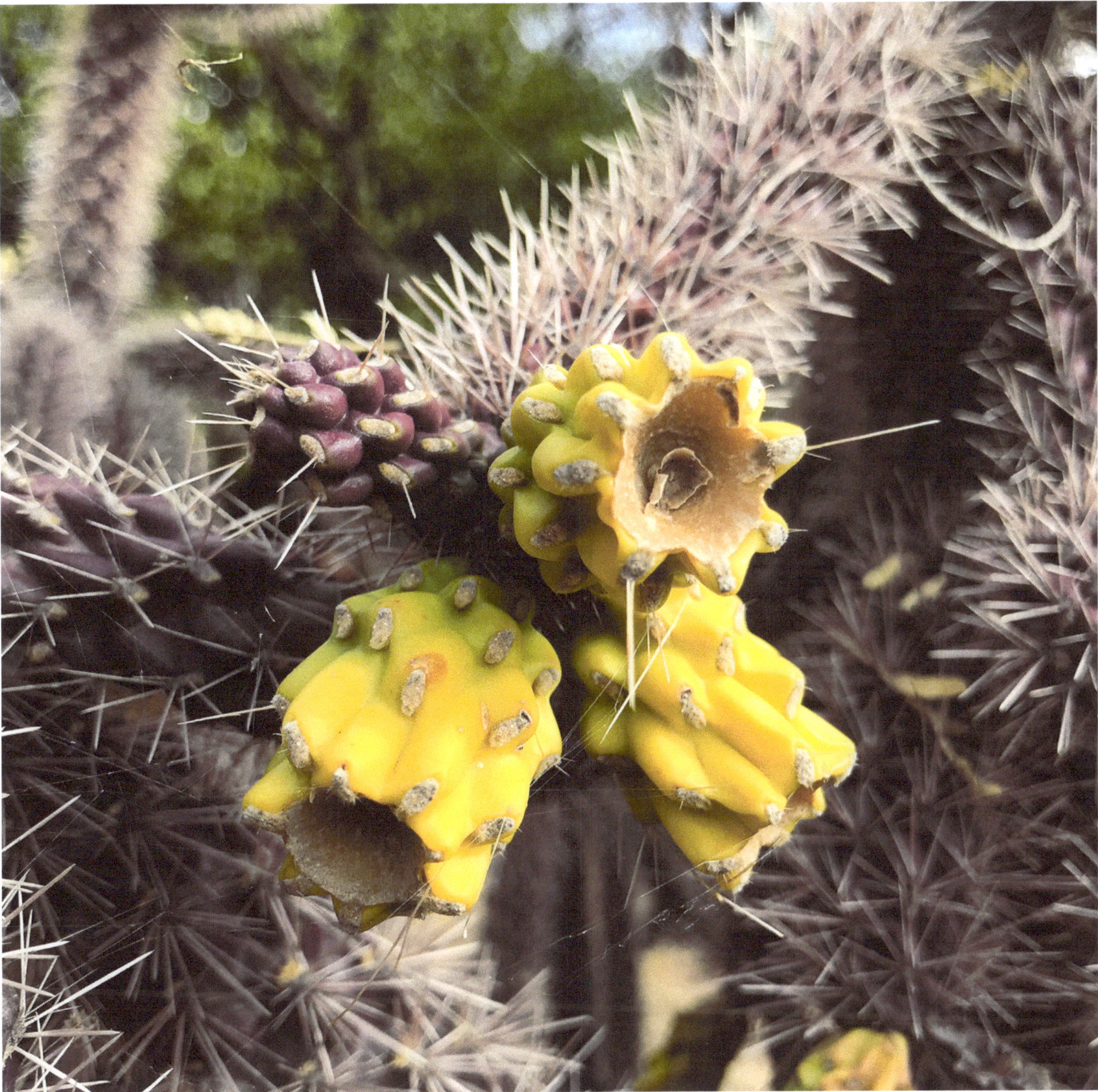

Separation: A Moment with...

Lovers gaze at their future,
while delighting hearts bond together.
Closeness is felt through the mind,
body and soul as their spirits remain forever.

One day builds upon another
with bursts of joy and glory.
For them, life is blissful
as their bond is tight
and they trust this enchanted story.

Time and circumstances enter their lives
without fair warning to their hearts.
Others spread false rumors
for reasons of envy while tearing lives apart.

Separation and anxiety run through their minds as
communication is involuntarily blocked.
Desperate for answers leads to
vulnerability creating dubious thoughts.

Finally, lovers discovered the trickery
of those with cruel intentions.
Forever exposed, the malicious ones
can never inflict evil again.

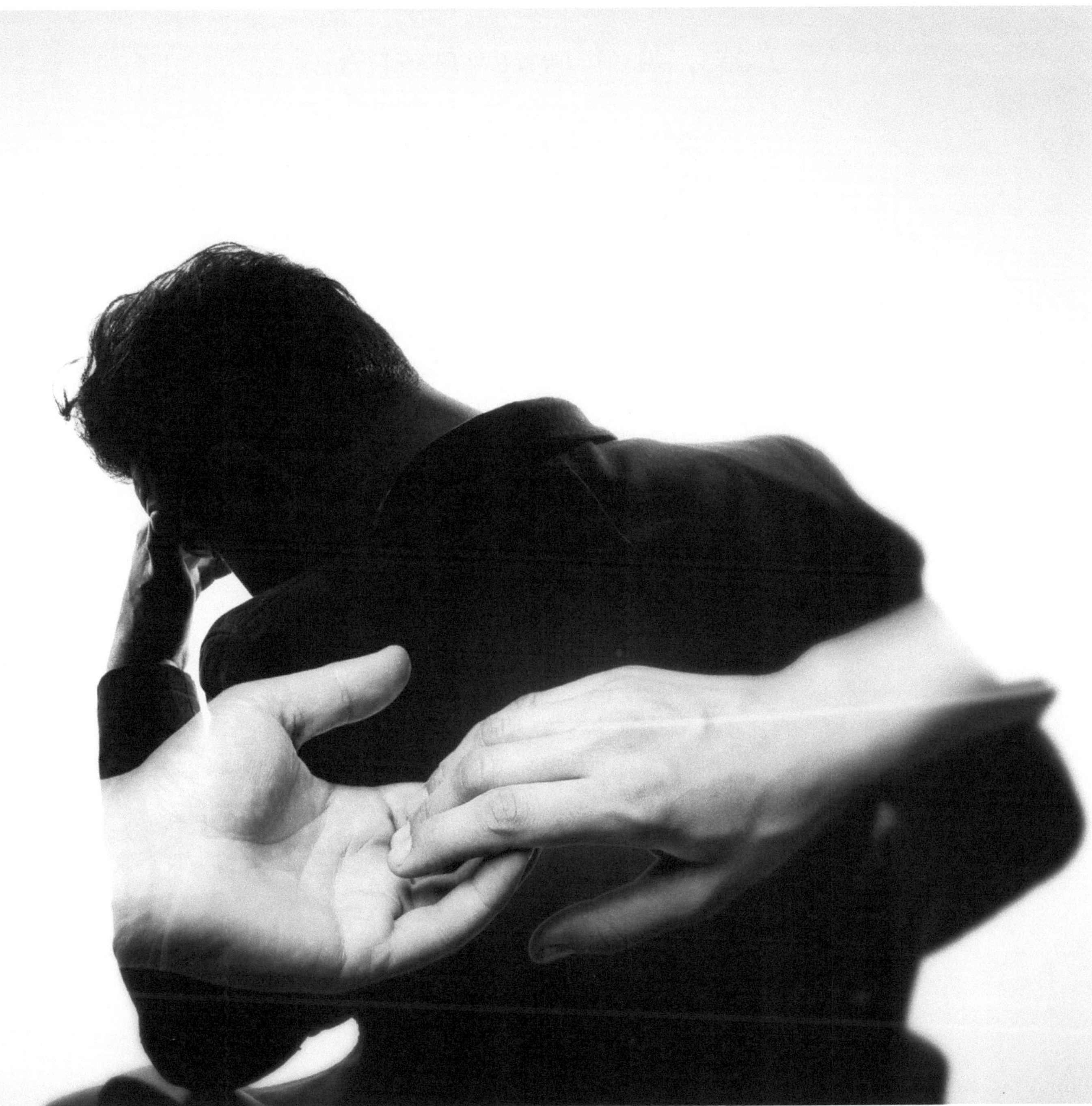

Loss: A Moment with...

Loss is life's mystery
as to why it must occur.
Circumstances don't match
what we would prefer.

Memories of others
are part of our life,
yet they don't make sense
during dark times of strife.

Try not to dwell
on what's no longer present,
as it brings down the spirit
into feeling unpleasant.

It takes loss to know
what you treasure and fear,
but know to stay calm
for a gift will appear.

Hold strong and save the treasures
of those whom you still care,
but know when to let go
if it's no longer shared.

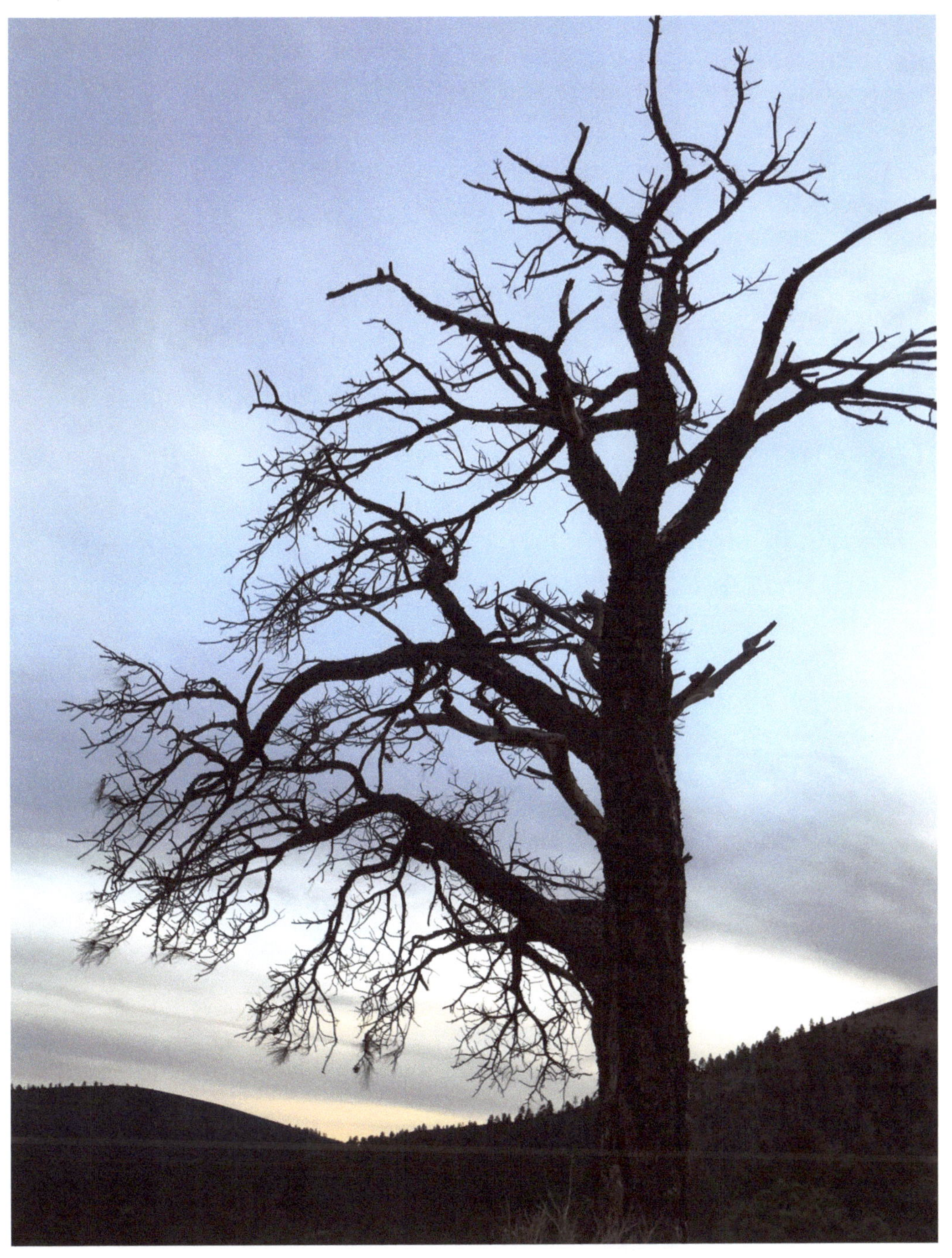

Forgiveness: A Moment with…

Forgiveness is the answer to life's pain;
so, forgive yourself and each other the same.

The words seem so simple and may be easy to say;
yet, only your heart can show you the way.

You're haunted by memories and words such "if only".
Our past needs acceptance so as not to feel lonely.

Are forgiving and forgetting two words that are the same?
Your answer will tell you when there is no more shame.

So let go of it all and treat yourself well,
Forgiveness is finished when you can no longer tell.

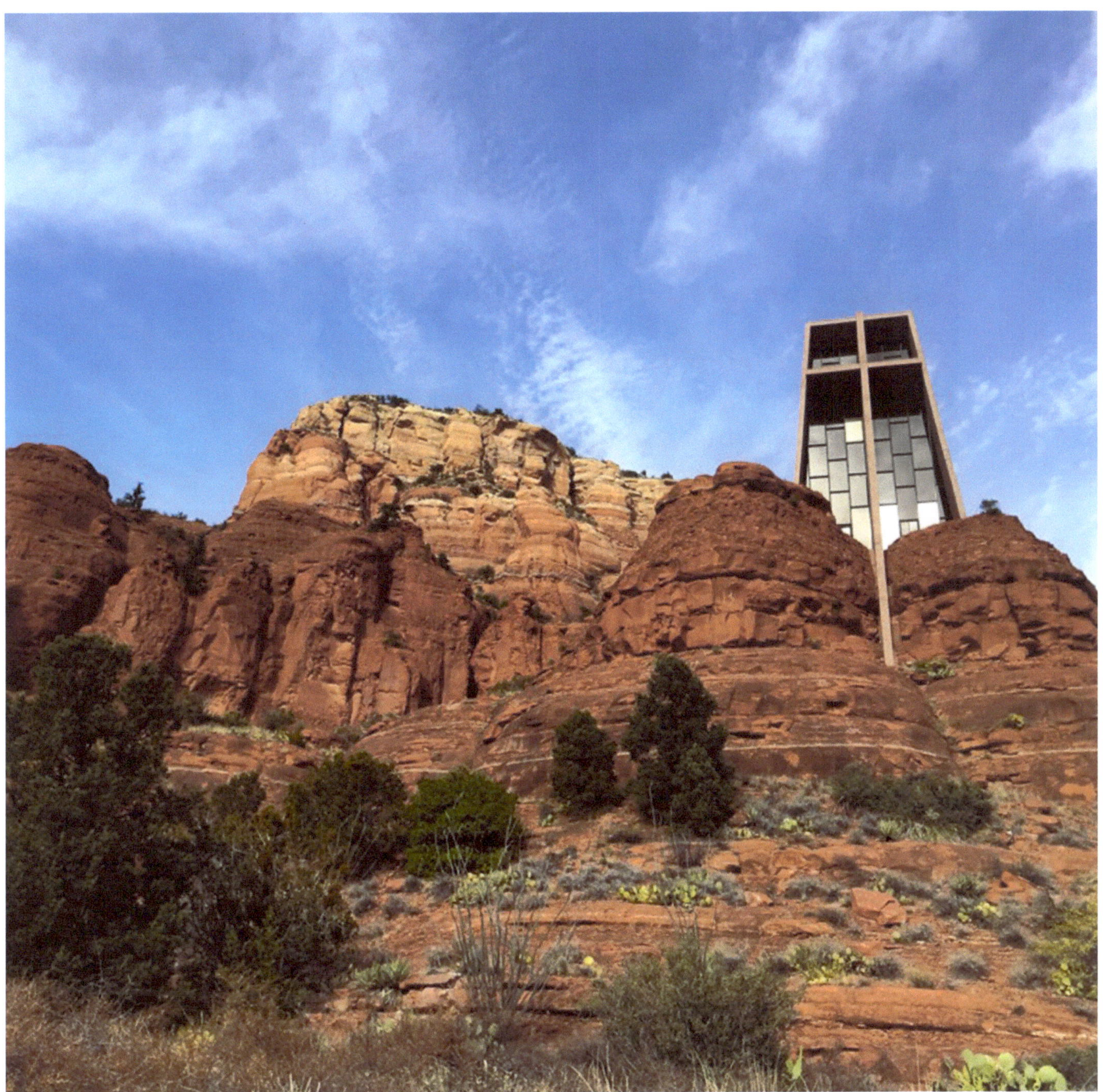

Innocence of Children: A Moment with...

Young children are innocent as to what they say.
They discover life by learning through play.

Their smiles and laughter and their trust in all
is refreshing to us, as we recognize their call.

They believe with a pure heart
and their spirit is untainted,
as they inform us with delightful
uncensored information.

They make us laugh as they have natural humor.
They are placed here for our very own future.

Children are blessings and their stage is alive,
yet sadly they grow to be skeptics
through the trials of adult life.

If the world were run by children's rules,
there would be no discretions.
That is why life must teach them
a variety of lessons.

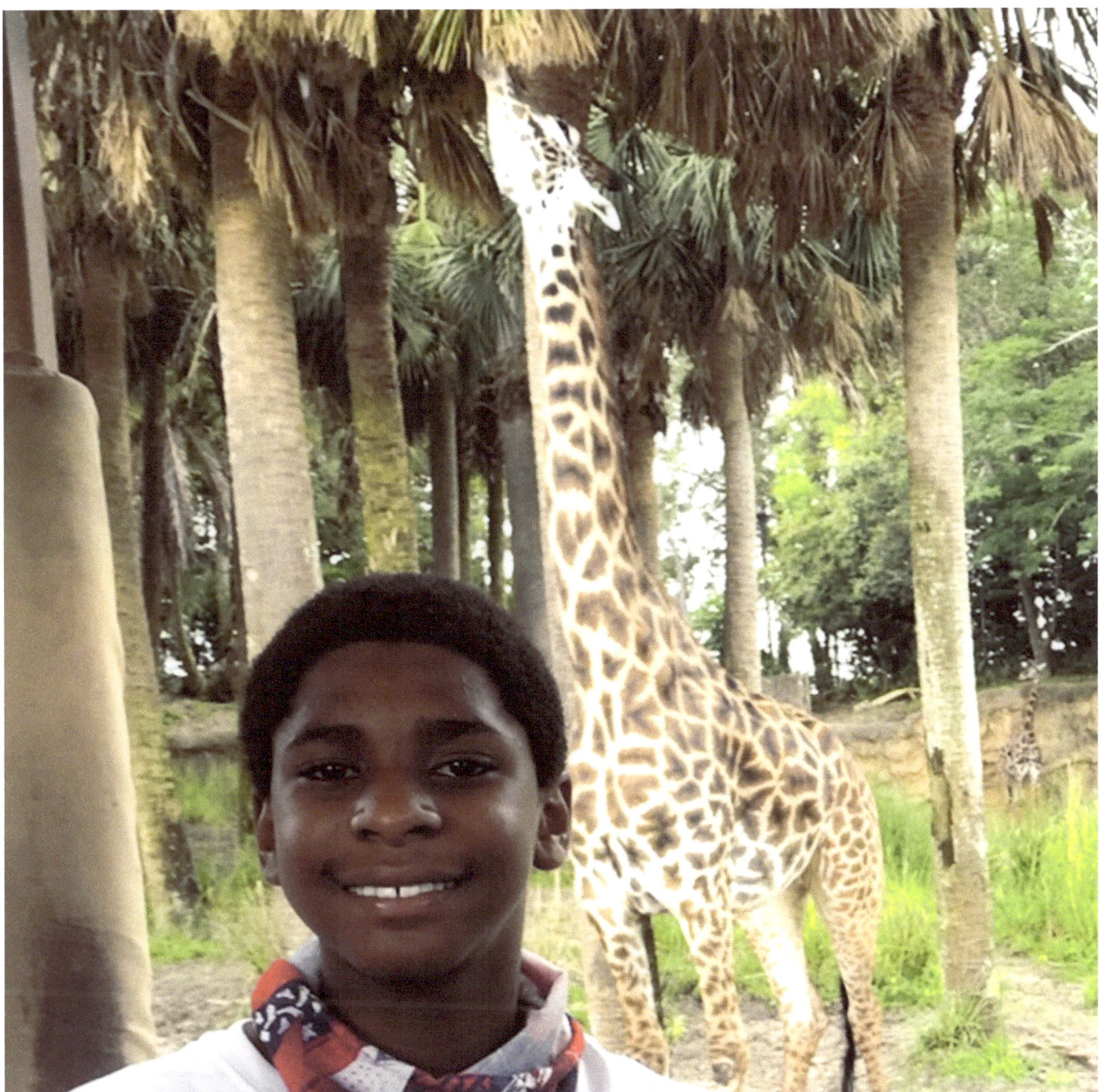

Love: A Moment with...

Love grows as it's given away.
The more you give
the happier you'll stay.

Love is fragile,
so handle with care.
Be gentle to others
so it can always be shared.

Love is honesty and trust
should be treasured,
for love is a gift
that cannot be measured.

If you are with someone
and love flies away,
let go of the inevitable
but lead not astray.

Let yourself love deeply
running straight from your heart.
Never give up on it because
the Spirit has a part.

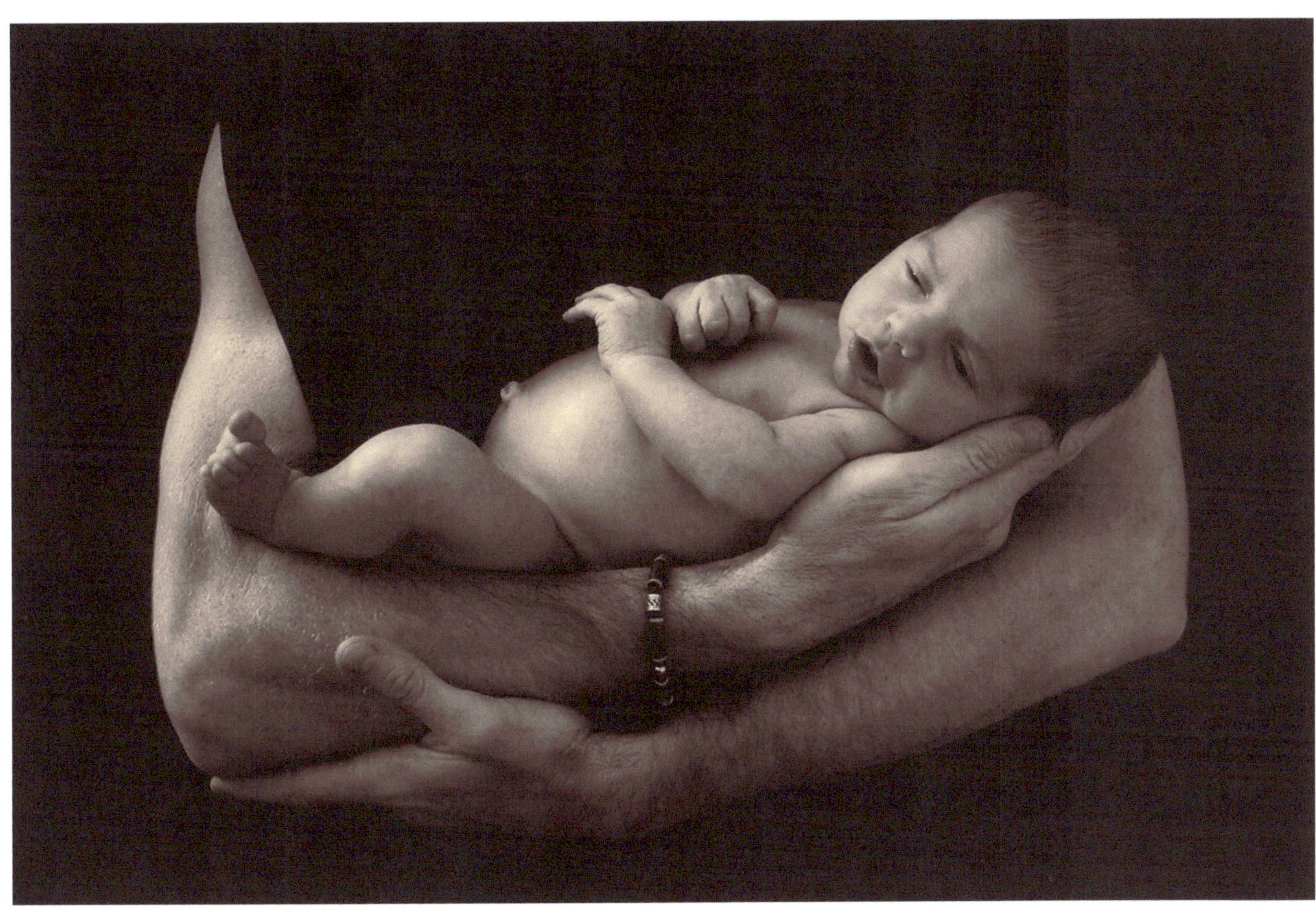

Employment: A Moment with...

Employment should of course
include great ration;
yet, greed can't bond with loyalty,
or human compassion.

God hears our needs
and those with whom we work.
Narcissism is dangerous,
so be cautious with your actions
as well as with your words.

Working should be reciprocal
where care is number one.
Let a piece of your reward embrace
the needs of everyone.

Employment is a necessity,
but shouldn't take advantage of others;
so, use your gifts to help our sisters and brothers.

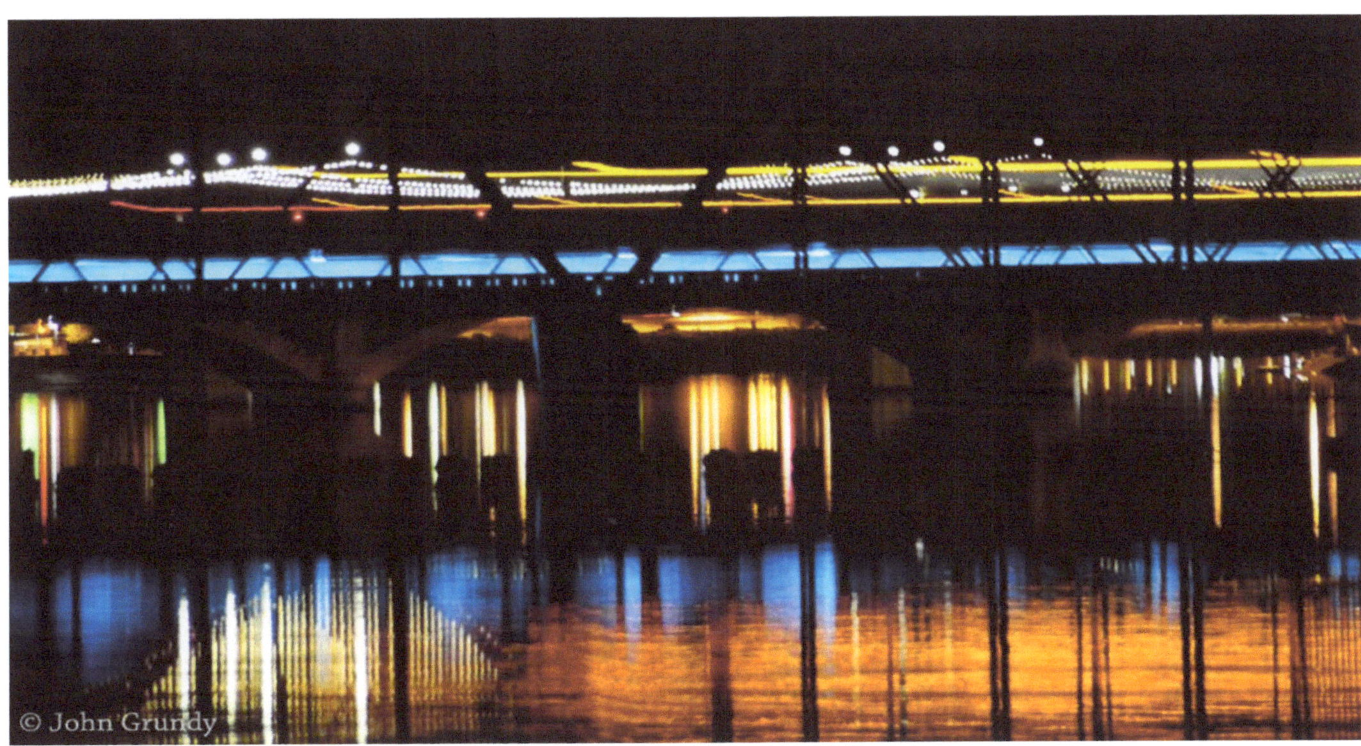
© John Grundy

The Sea: A Moment with...

Glistening waters are in hues of blue and green.
You can wade in shallow waters
that are clear and pristine.

Deeper waters capture darker shades.
One can view the white caps from cascading waves.

A whole world lives under the sea,
including schools of fish
under coral reefs, and sea anemone.

Return to the shoreline while riding the waves.
Feel the crunchy sand between your toes,
as you bob out of the foam feeling amazed.

Relax and smell the salt air
while observing the ebb and flow of the tide.
The crashing waves melt onto the shoreline
as it keeps the beaches alive.

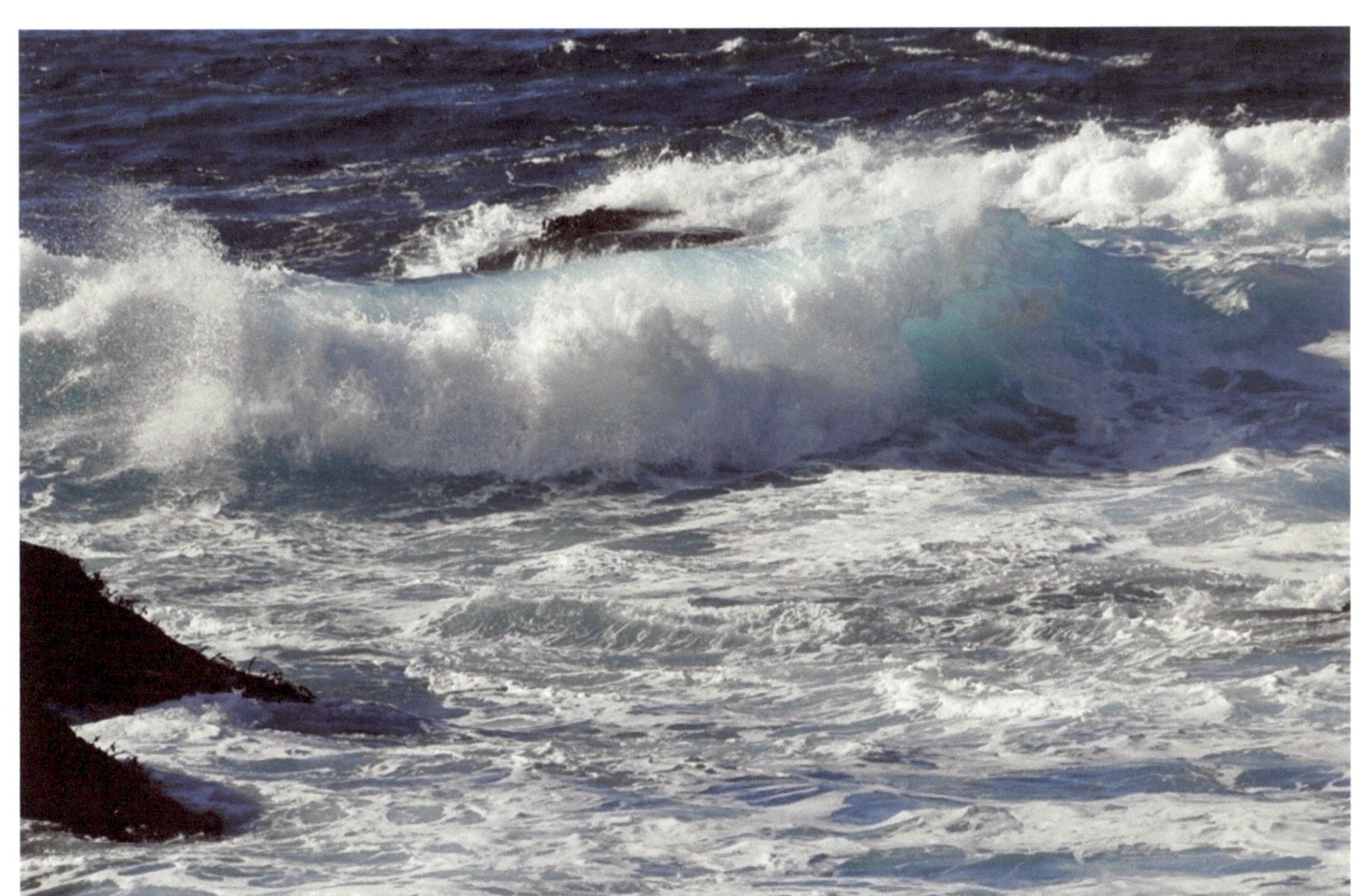

Listen to Your Calling:
A Moment with...

The beginning was a seed
to which God brought forth a root.

Each raindrop of experiences
nourished it to shoot.

Inspired by an Order,
the shoot began to bud.

He filled my heart with patience and
surrounded me with love.

Driven by results,
the roots spread far and wide.

Until the day my heartbeat stopped,
the field still alive.

Enjoy the blossoms of each day,
yet hold the petals falling.
For the roots are deep,
and the soul lives on...
So listen to your calling.

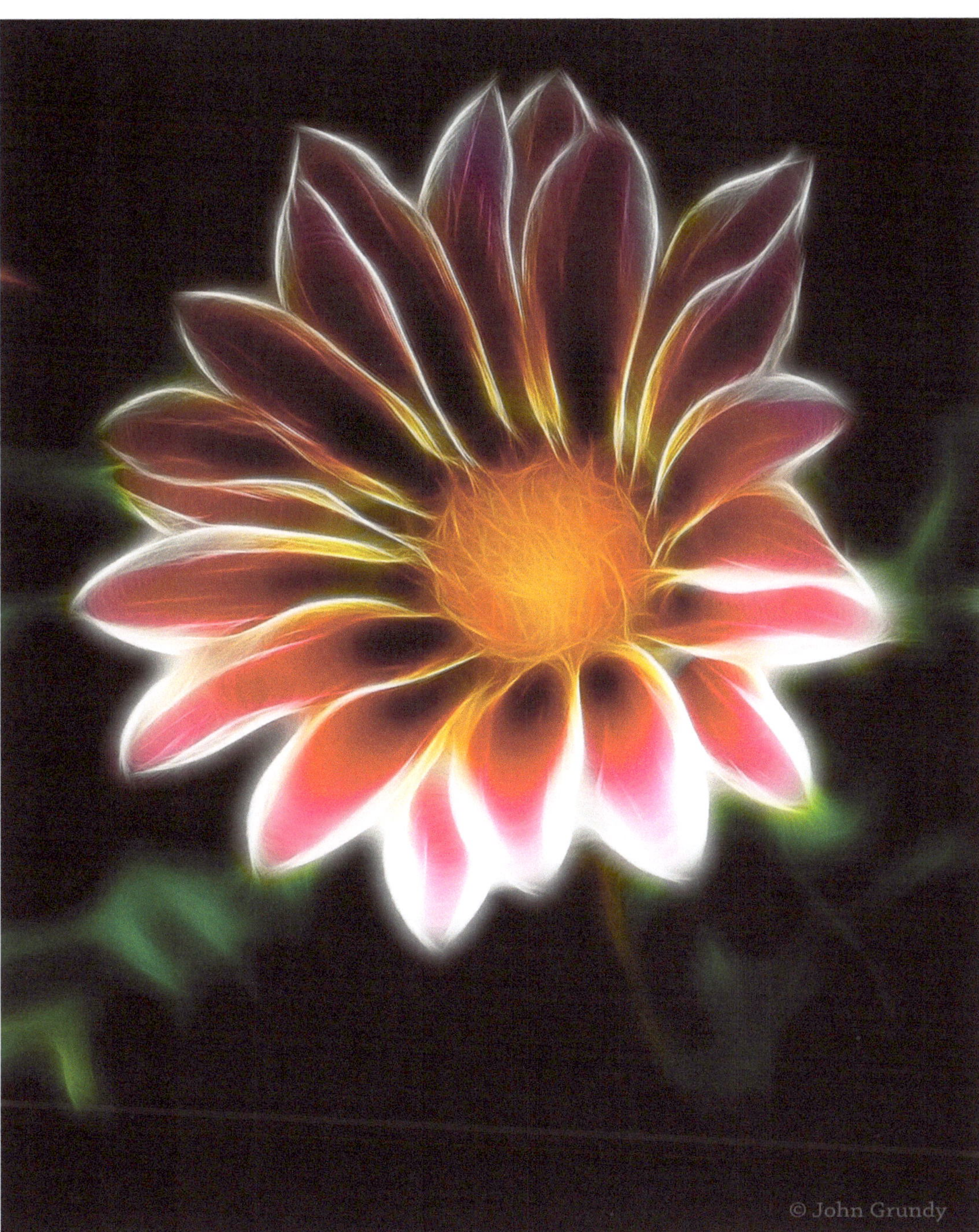
© John Grundy

Letting Go: A Moment with...

Letting it go is the key to life.
Gaze at the sunset through the trees at night.

Letting it go enables you to forgive;
by doing so allows others to live.

Letting it go generates gladness,
yet holding on to misunderstandings blocks
the perception of one's happiness.

Letting it go requires timing and patience.
Let's feel the quietness it brings
without maintenance.

Letting it go will set yourself free,
just accept one another and you shall soon see.

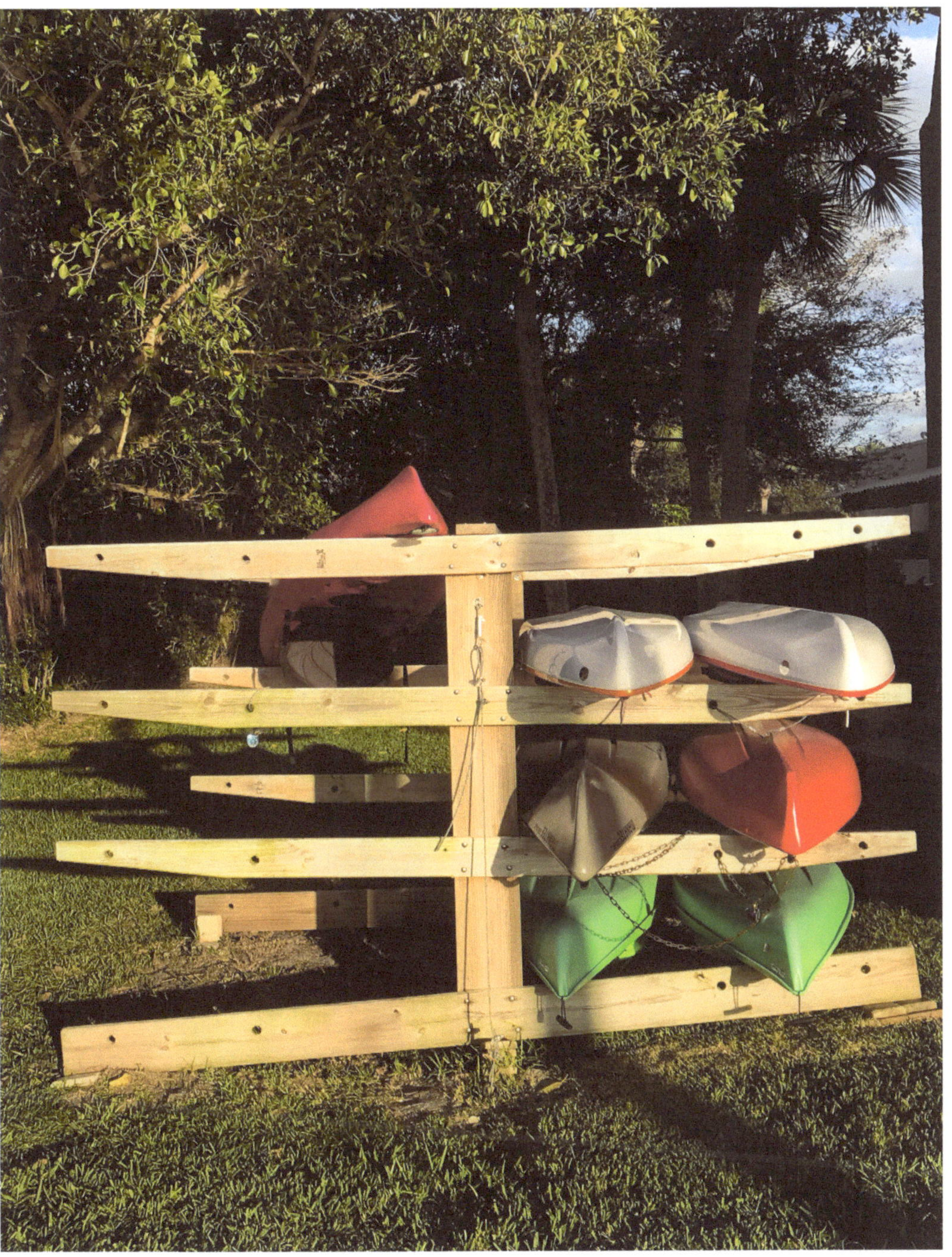

The Mind: A Moment with...

*Our brain houses pathways for memories
to be created,
yet our mind lets us travel
through what is mysteriously dated.*

*Neurons are electrically excitable as
their synaptic connections transfer through the cortex.
The mind is like a whirlpool spinning like a vortex.*

*New sensory and motor pathways stimulate neuroplasticity.
Treatment strategies are there to be put into place.*

*Oh, take me to a place where I shall feel safe.
Help me trace memories that are complex to embrace.*

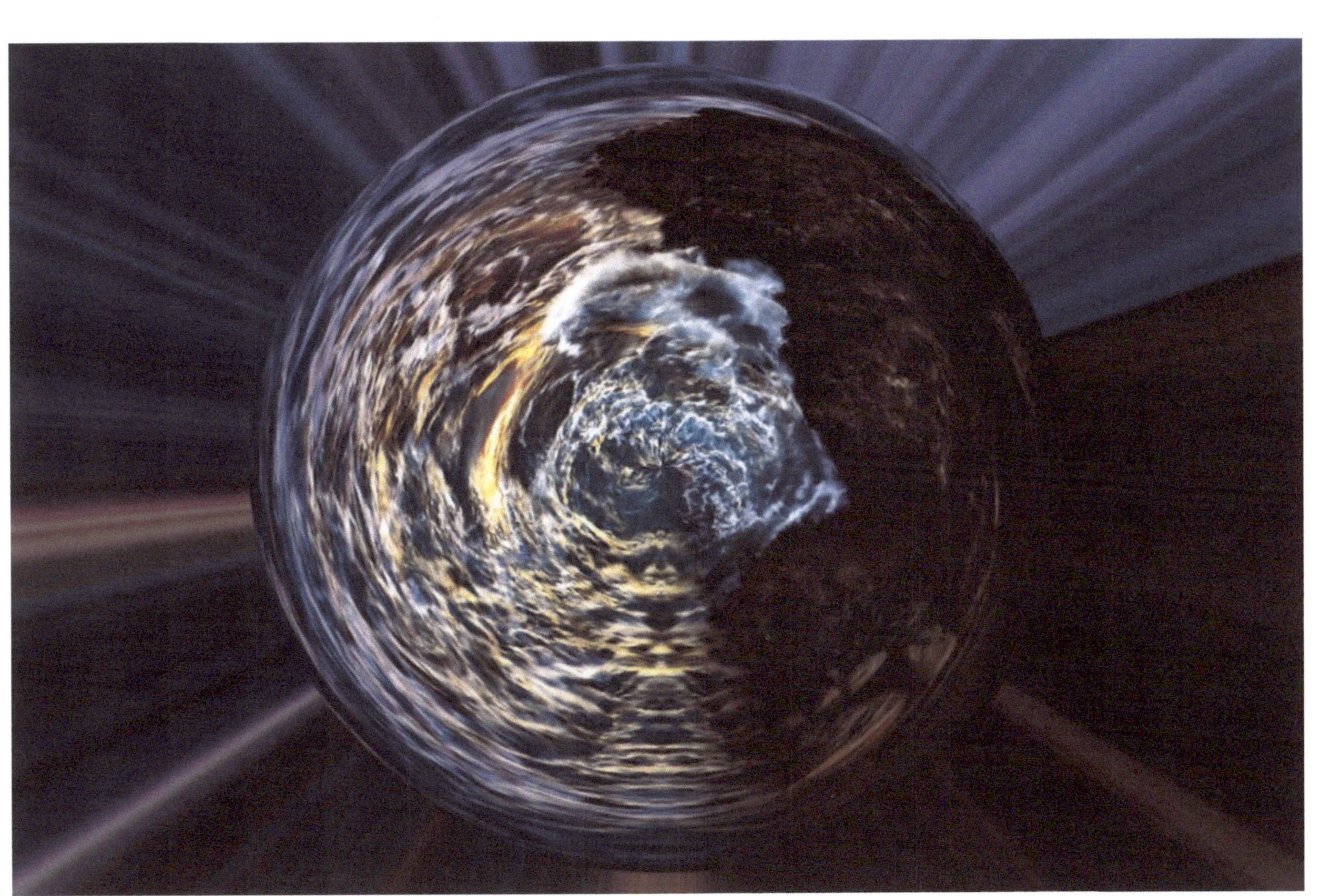

Understanding - A Balancing Act
A Moment with...

We can't always understand people and their actions;
yet, we can refrain from judgement and what
we perceive as infractions.

Don't wait until you understand
before moving forward in your life,
just trust that your acceptance
will bring equilibrium to what's right.

Forgiveness and patience
will help you find your way.
Balance your thoughts so
acceptance can stay.

Understanding yourself is the best path;
so, balance life's relationships
from now till we pass.

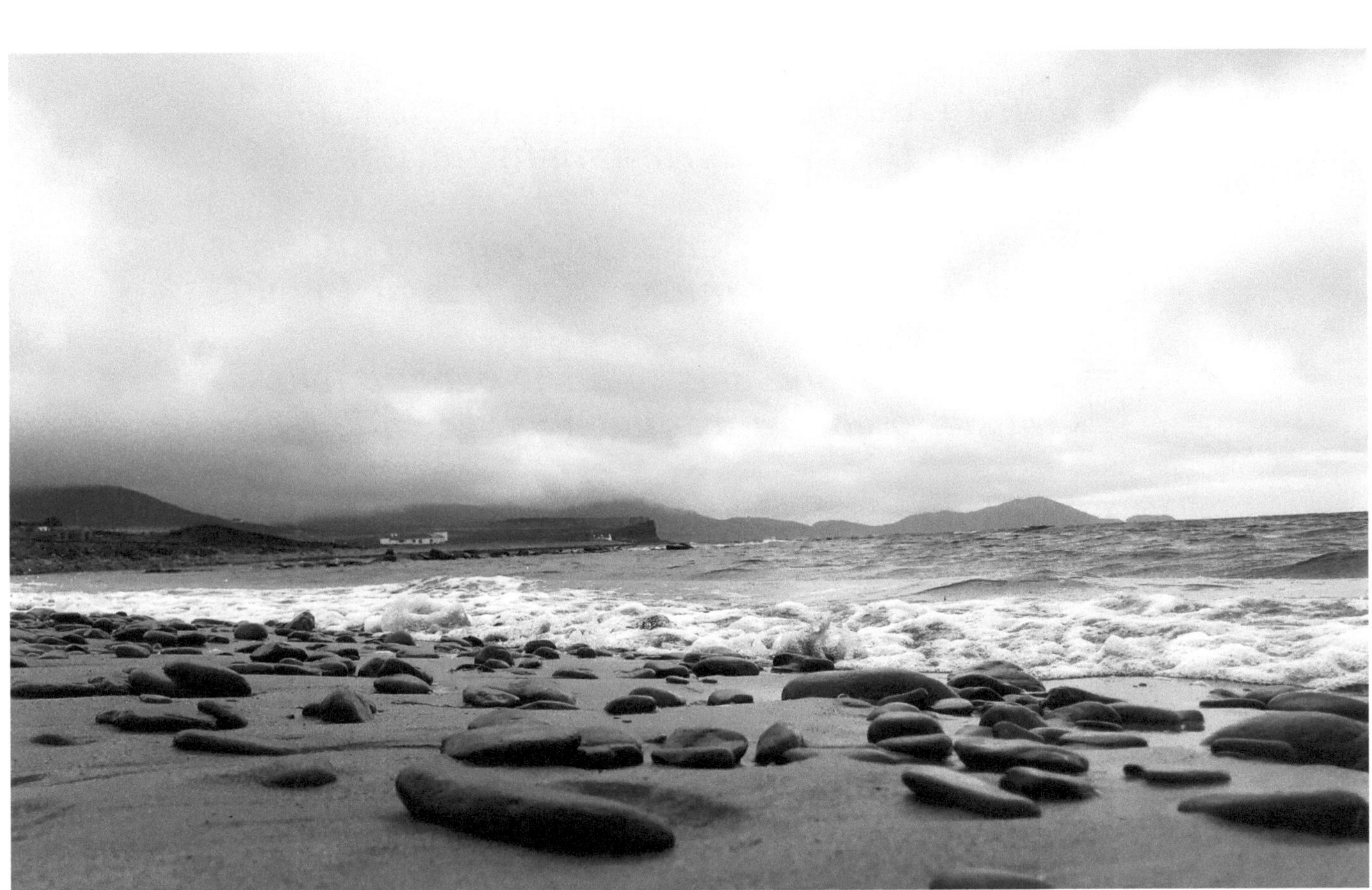

Music to Your Ears:
A Moment with...

Melody and harmony create a fine tune.
Listen to the music from night until noon.

A cappella or instrumental to your ears delight,
creating a thirst for music that feels just right.

Strings and percussions and the beat to follow,
is music to your ears that is never hollow.

The piano and organ, the cello played with emotion,
gives your spirit a time for peaceful devotion.

Don't forget bells and the ringing of chimes,
or the free flowing sounds that nature provides.

Music to your ears doesn't have to be heard,
but instead it's a feeling when it is observed.

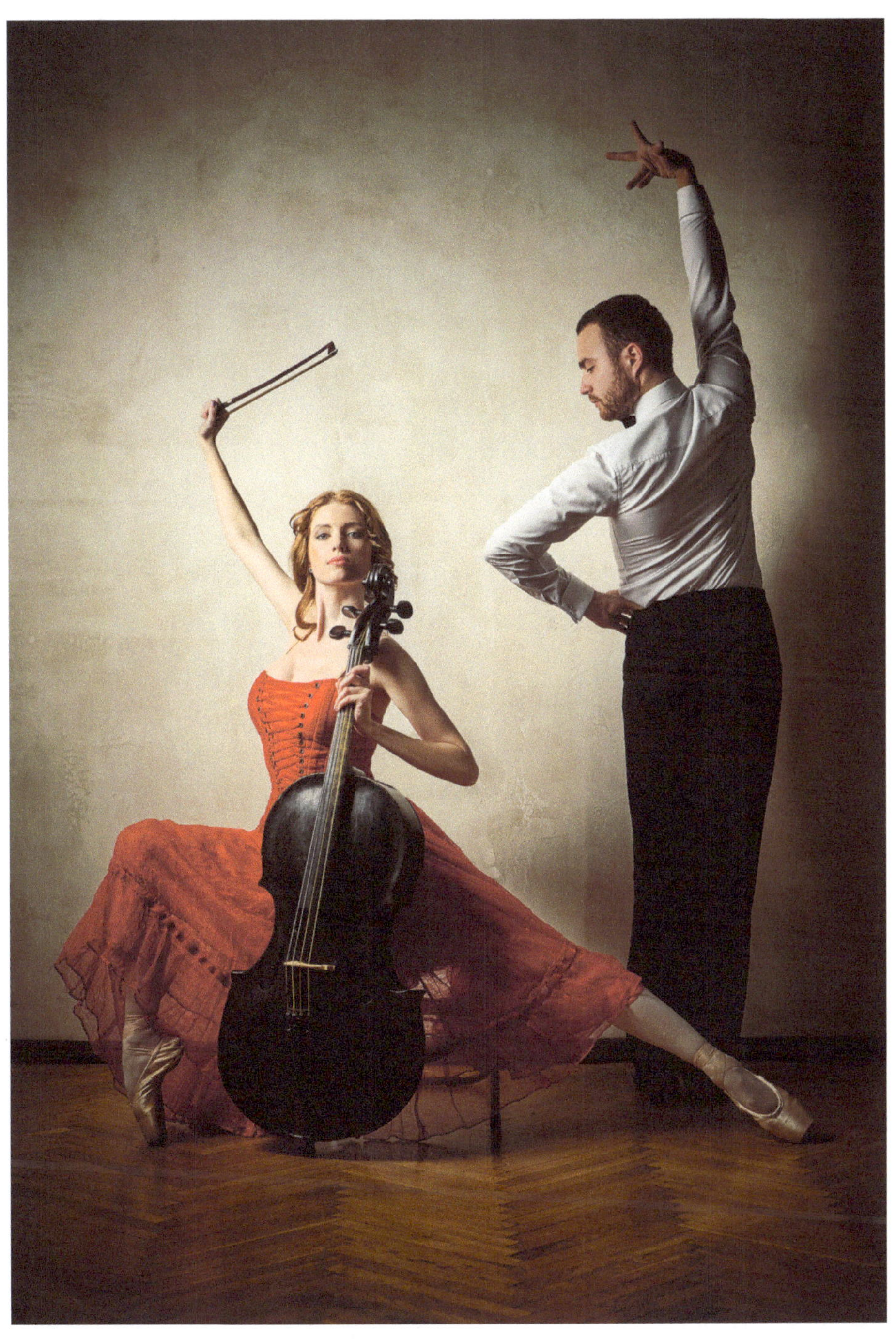

Perception: A Moment with…

We perceive information
through our unique set of lenses.
This is how interpretation leads us
to our beliefs and deceptions.

Factors that alter
how one perceives information,
include the need for sensory integration.

Perception is crucial
as it's resulting force determines
the outcome of each of our reactions.
Cultural influences encourage respect,
tolerance and our unique set
of personal satisfactions.

If the universe steered us
in the same direction,
there would be nothing unique
about our own perception.

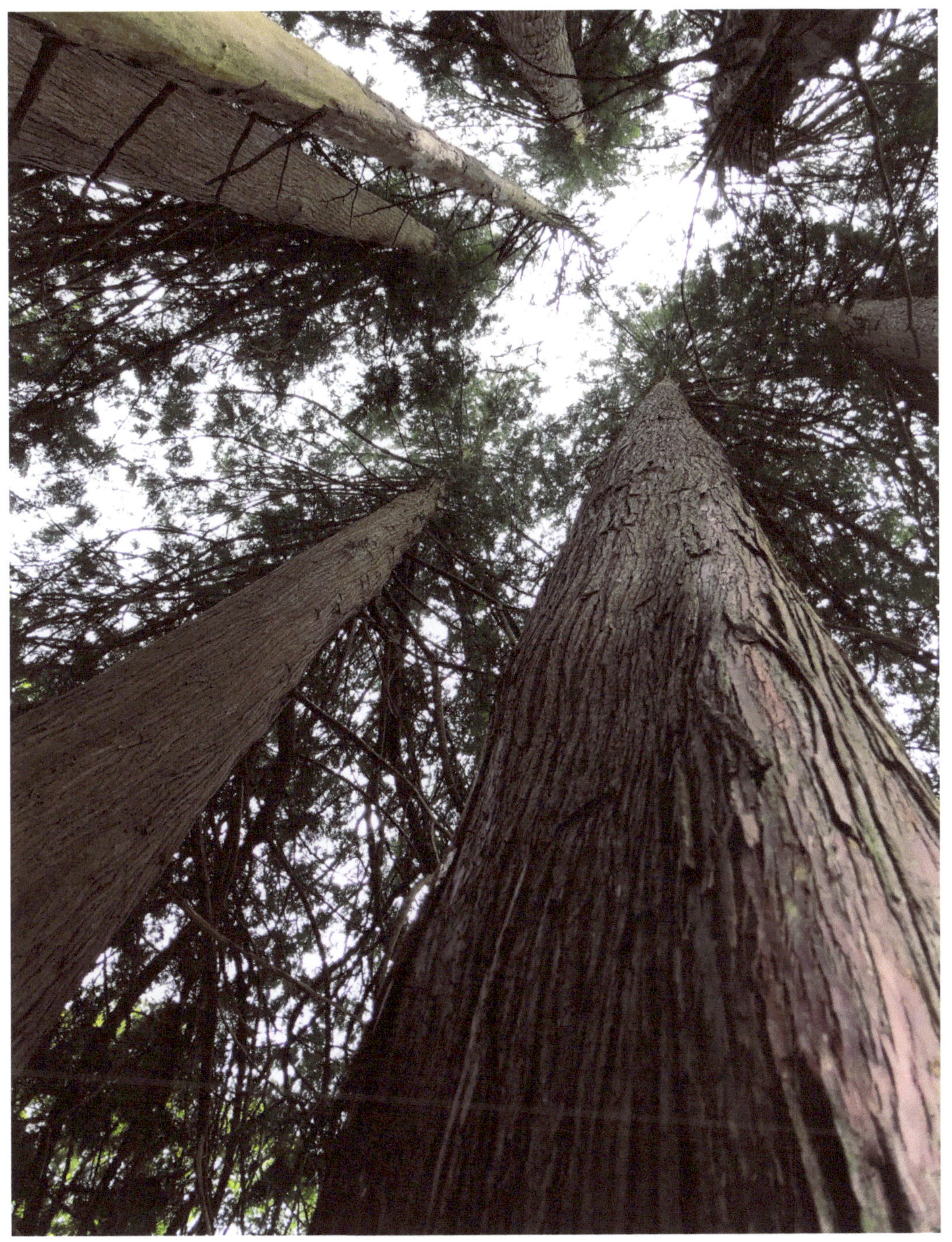

Wind: A Moment with...

Wind sounds different
depending upon where one hears it.
It is silent without barriers and
ears to perceive it.

A gentle breeze whispers
through the pines,
while their cones dance
with needles under the sun that shines.

Wind currents from a gale-storm
create swishing like tunes,
until its orchestra dominates
the shoreline and its dunes.

Listen to the wind-chimes
in your own secret garden.
Feel your heart beat
as the wind speaks its pardon.

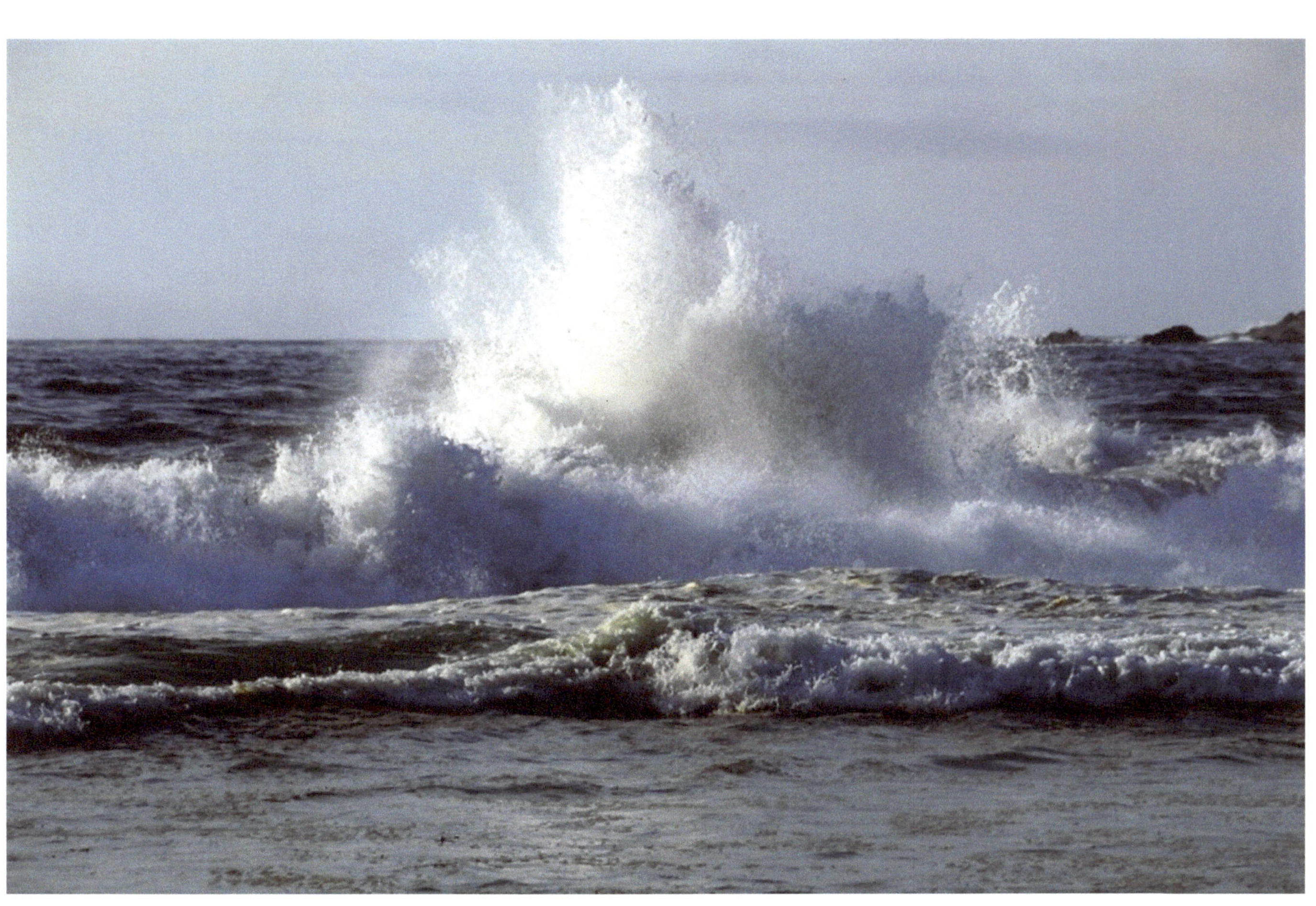

Masks: A Moment with...

Masks change the perception of how others view us.
They are subconsciously worn to conceal a weakness.

We wear them to sustain us from becoming defensive,
while helping us from feeling too apprehensive.

Masks protect us from vulnerability,
while they are frequently worn to escape futility.

One may not realize they are wearing a mask,
as it is often worn to cover our past.

Self-confidence builds as one works through situations;
while finally learning to peel the layers
of our masks without trepidation.

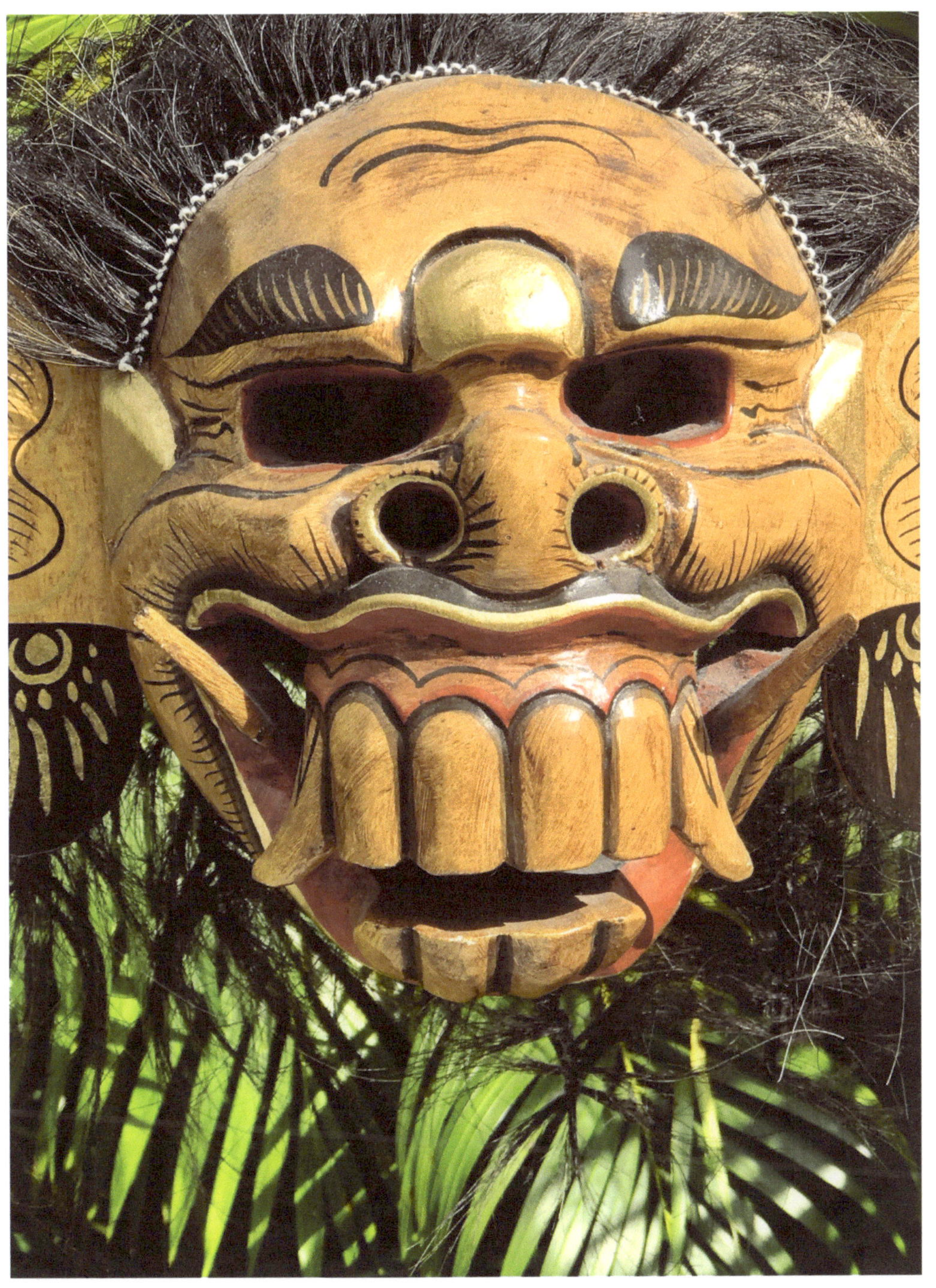

Journey: A Moment with...

Your senses will take you on a real life journey,
like roaming through the countryside when not in a hurry.

The waxing and waning of the moon brings soft light,
be sure to smell the scents that come out at night.

Sunsets across the water are simply serene,
while sunrise tomorrow is waiting to be seen.

Driving through mountain ranges
and fields of golden flowers;
one can feel serenity through ethereal powers.

Tasting the spices and drinking the wine,
fine food from other countries
will remind you of your time.

Hearing the raindrops and smelling the ozone;
admire the sparkling dew drops
on petals in the morning.

Life's experiences are unique to one's journey; so,
continue to collect memories into eternity.

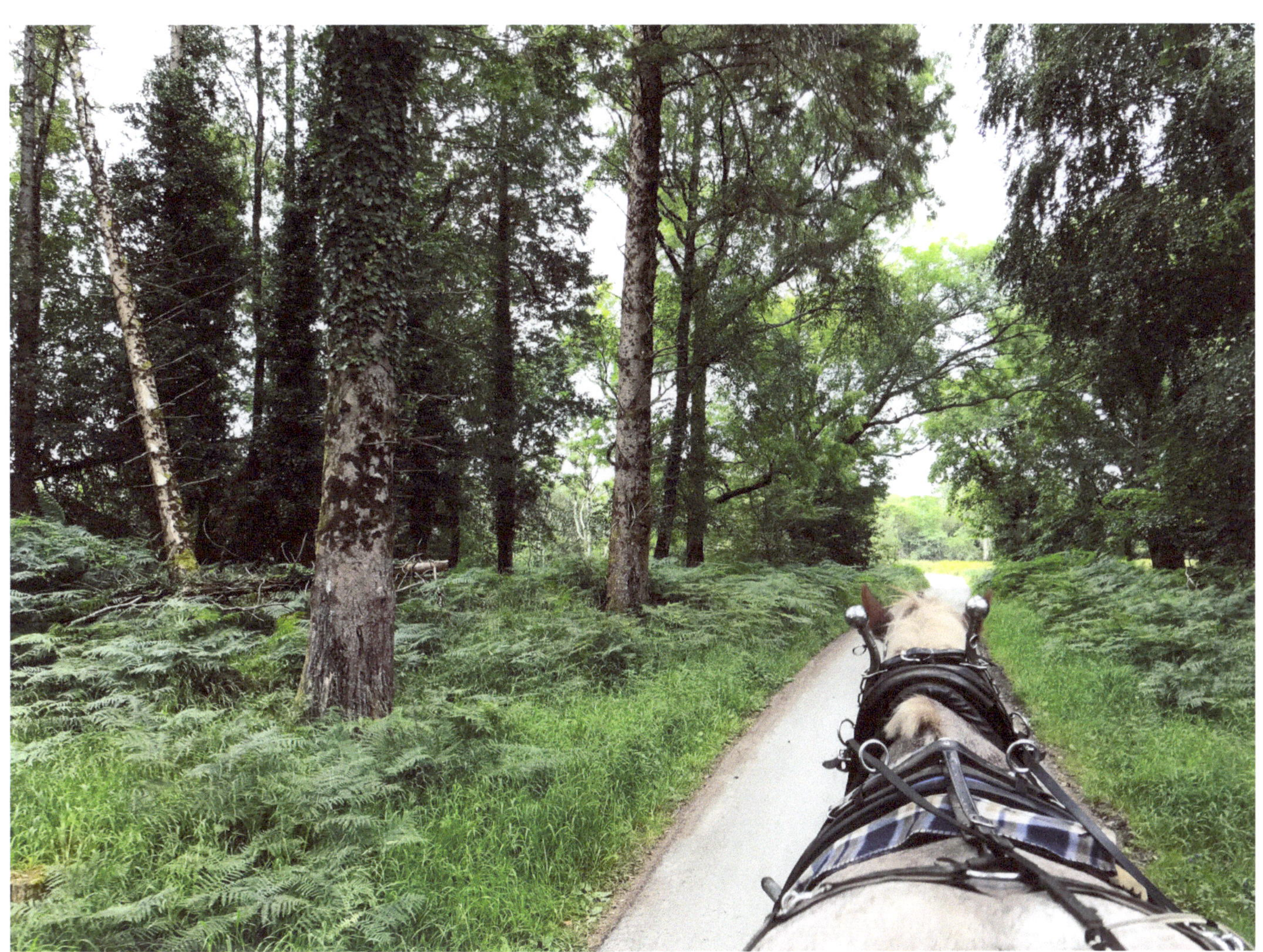

Happiness: A Moment with...

Happiness comes from the depth of one's soul;
yet, giving and benevolence
makes one whole.

Money and power are things that won't find it.
Pretending one is happy can only just hide it.

Happiness is a mindset that only you can create,
by giving and serving
and living your own faith.

How do you keep happiness from flying away?
By remembering gratitude
will keep it at bay.

Find your own happiness and don't let it go.
Be true to yourself
for it will continue to grow.

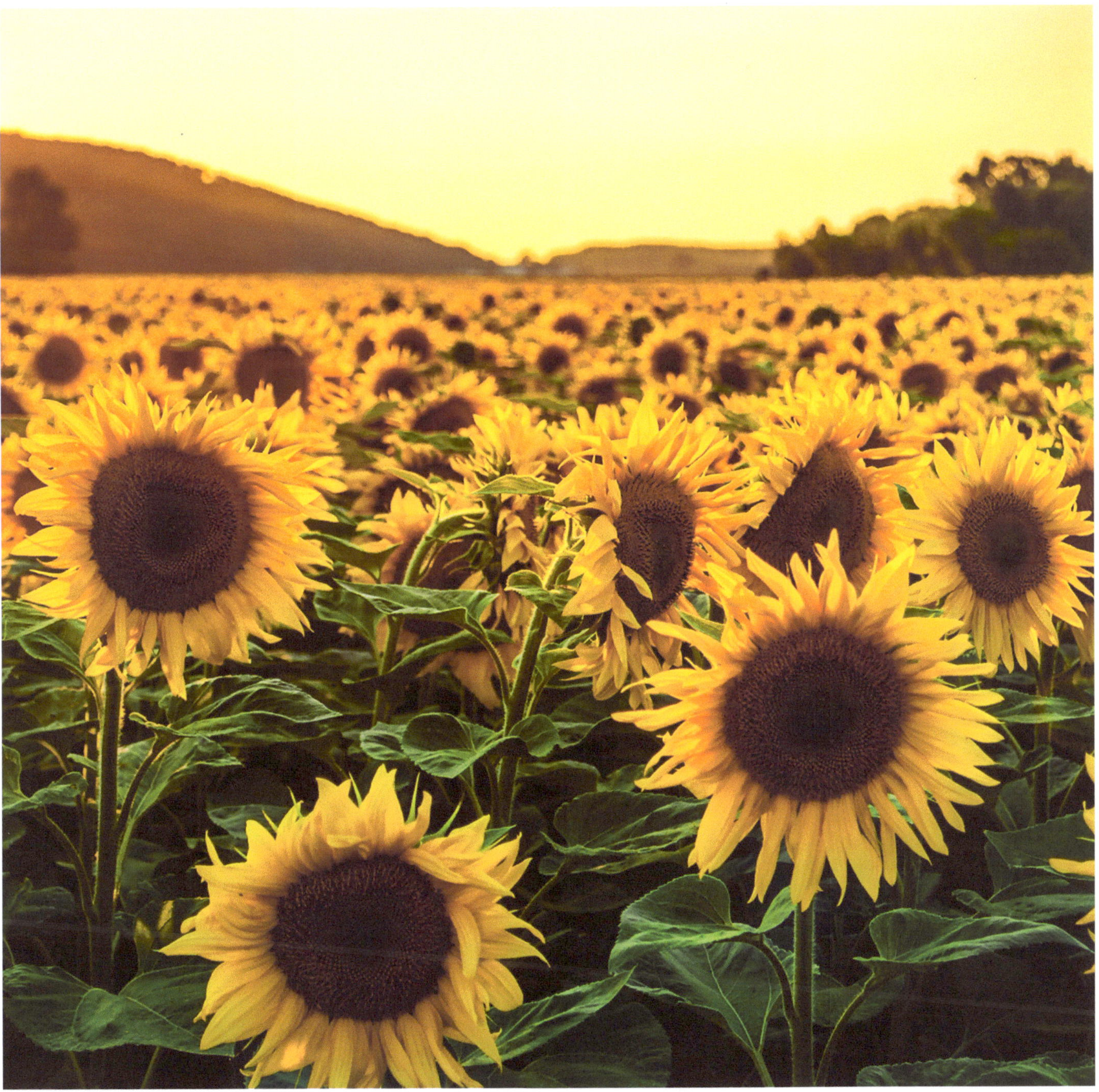

Disabilities: A Moment with...

Disabilities are abilities that are
yet to be tapped.
They are individualistic
and are able to be unwrapped.

Look for the "can do's" and build from there.
Look at the "can't do's" and target what's fair.

Search who can help
facilitate the uniqueness of one's needs.
Don't settle for less,
as a miracle can be seized.

Perfection might not happen;
yet, you are never alone.
Be creative with baby steps,
for God's plan is unknown.

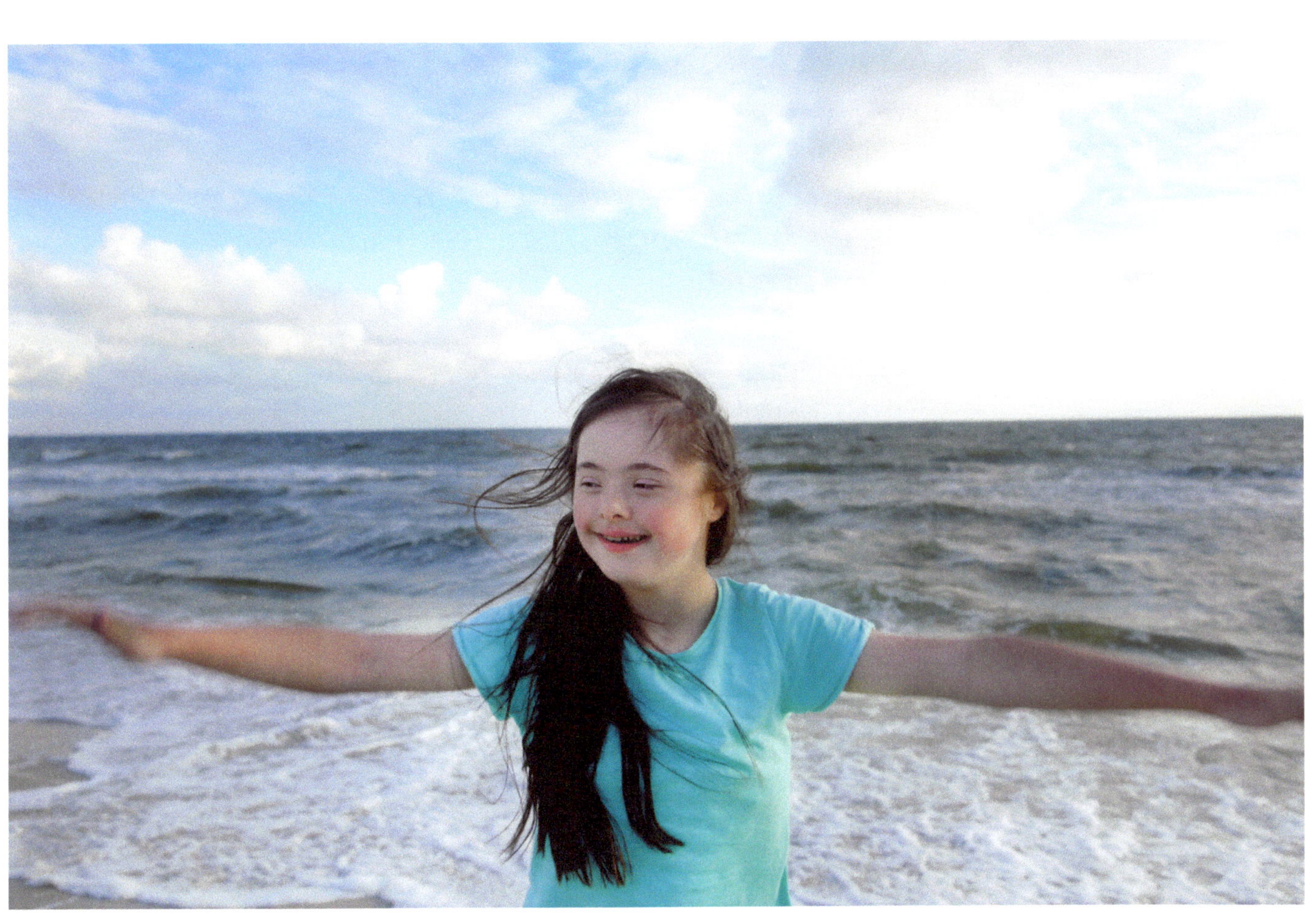

Hope: A Moment with...

Hope can persevere
during times that seem relentless.
Lean on your faith when you are hesitant.

No matter the experience
of what you're going through,
trust with all your strength that
the spirit lives within you.

Visualize what you need
and not just what you ask.
Give yourself permission
for all anxieties to pass.

Even at your worst,
know that One is present.
It is knowing and believing
that hope will reveal its essence.

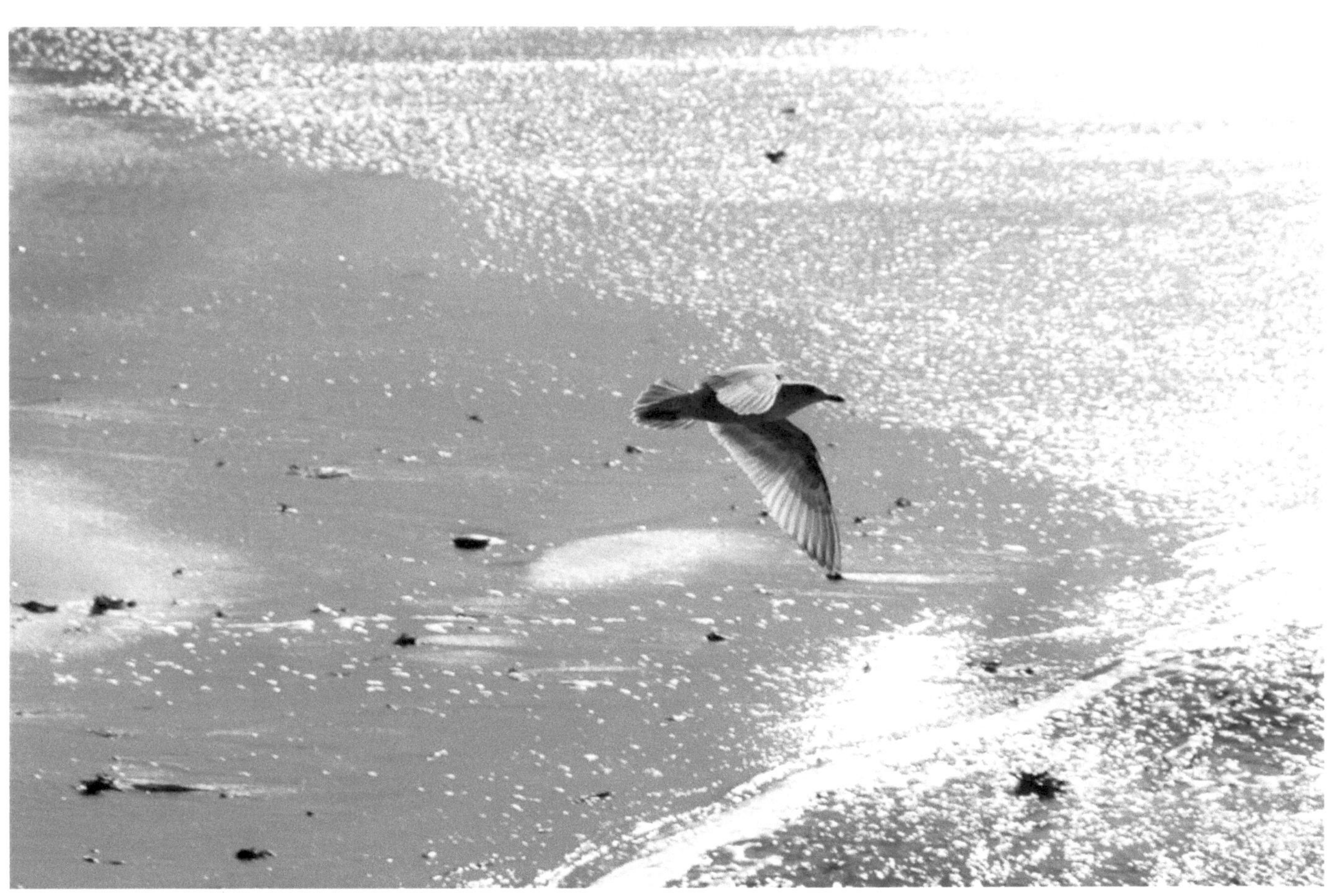

Disappointment: A Moment with...

It's alright to feel disappointed when situations come along.
We lean on what's right and accept what's wrong.

Relationships build and some do collapse.
It's normal to feel upset
when you can't walk out of the past.

Life seems unfair during tumultuous times.
There are no explanations that make it fine.

Anger must stop in order to heal,
so turn to the One that makes you feel real.

Life will resume its normal state,
as kindness and patience takes its place.

Stay alert to the process, it is never too late.
Treasure the moments when you feel safe.

Feelings will change as you grow a new life.
They may vacillate from forgiveness to feelings of strife.

Capture the half moon and follow its shadows.
Its peaceful guidance will lead you to Claddagh.

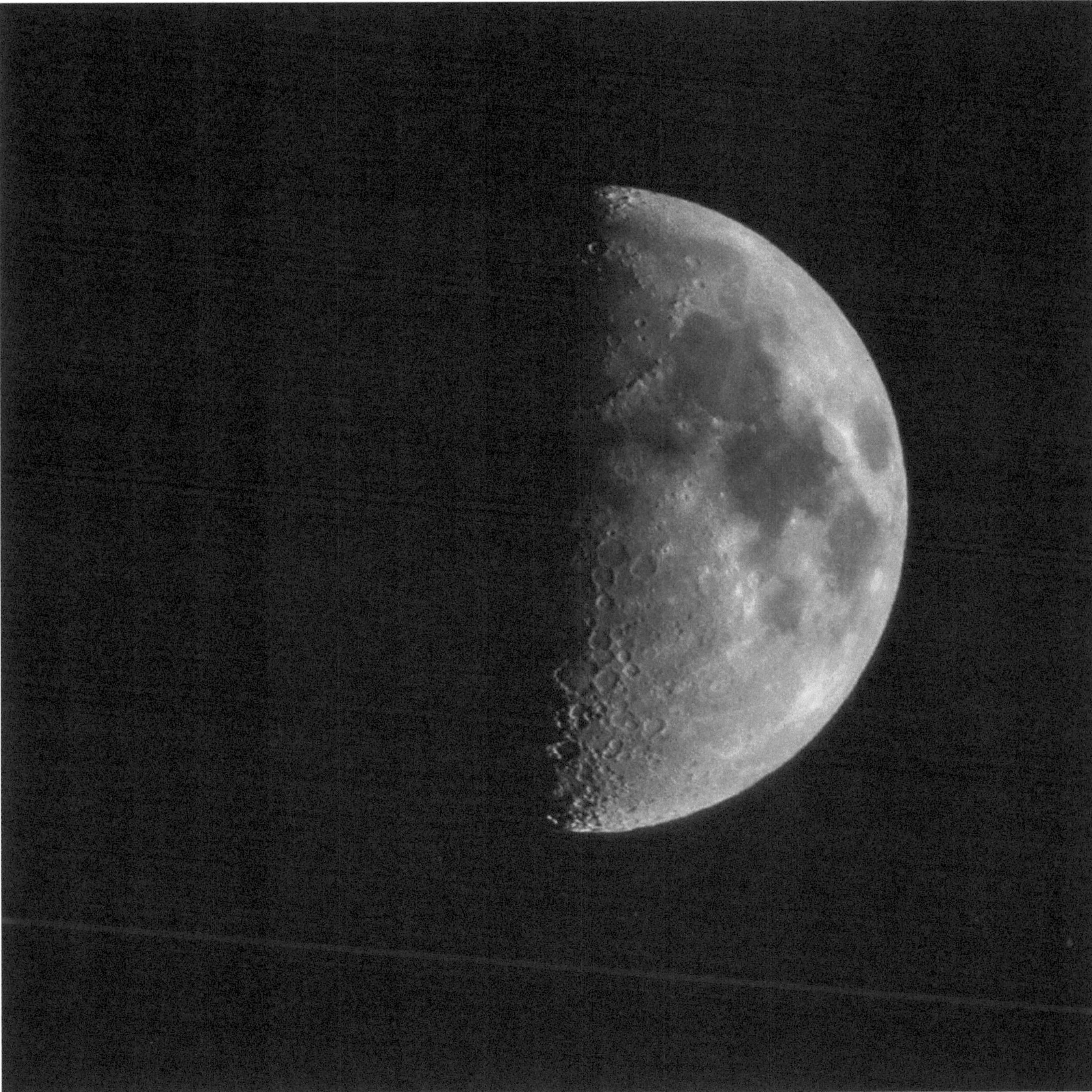

Wisdom: A Moment with...

What is wisdom and
from where does it come?
Its answer lies under
your very own thumb.

It's not what you're taught and
it's not what is solely schooled.
It is something you learn
from your experiences pooled.

Learn from mistakes,
but don't let yourself sink.
Sagacity is needed
to reflect upon what you think.

Don't ever take
your own wisdom for granted,
instead let the mind
be effectively planted.

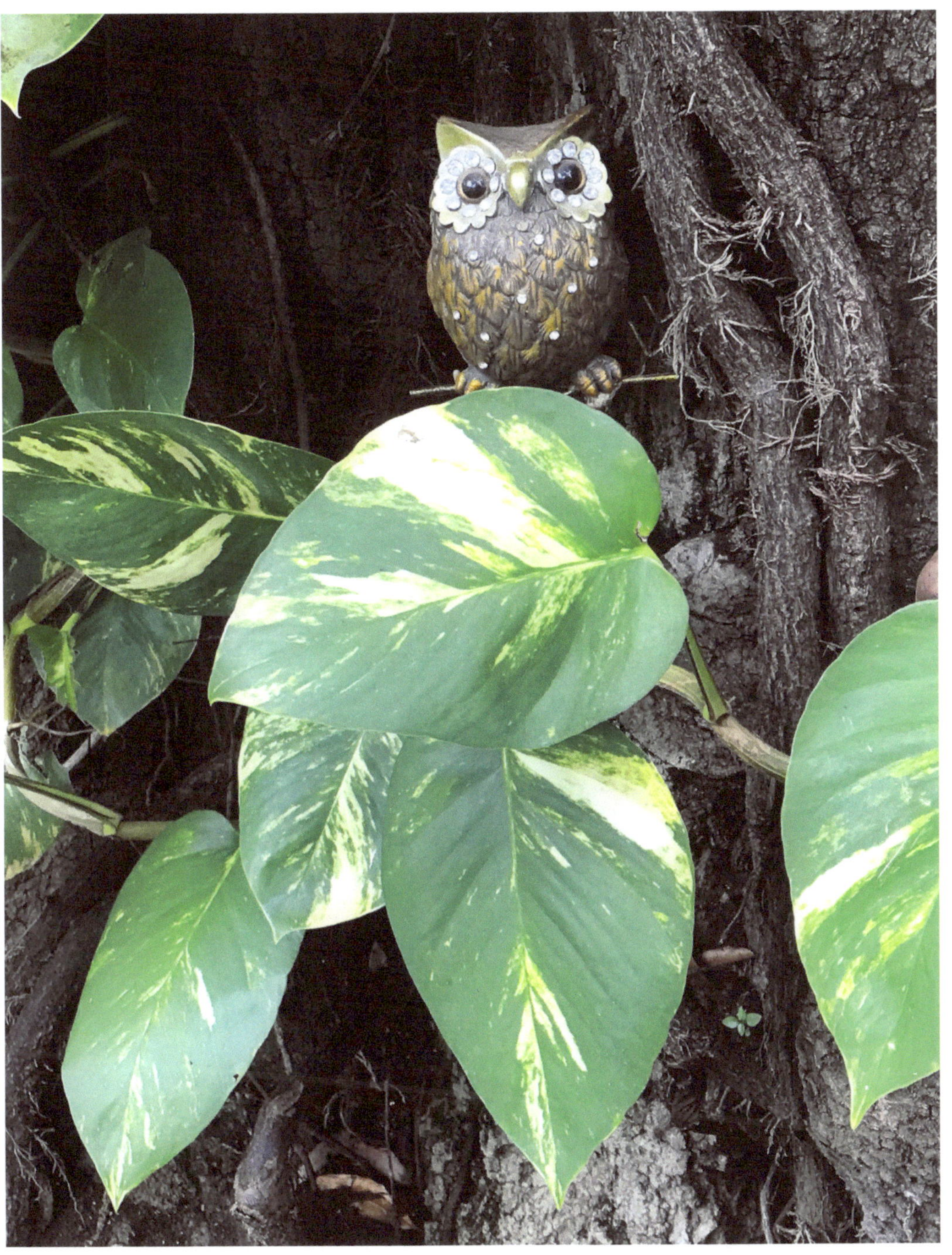

Joy: A Moment with...

Feel joyful with what you have,
as it could always be worse.
Feel joy in the heart even when it hurts.

Get that joy from way down deep,
dig it up even if it's a feat.

Catch it and hold it as closely as you can.
Place it in your mind to effectively stand.

Joy is something that is very contagious,
so surround yourself with those who are vivacious.

Don't let circumstances deprive you of joy.
Strike back against what makes you feel too coy.

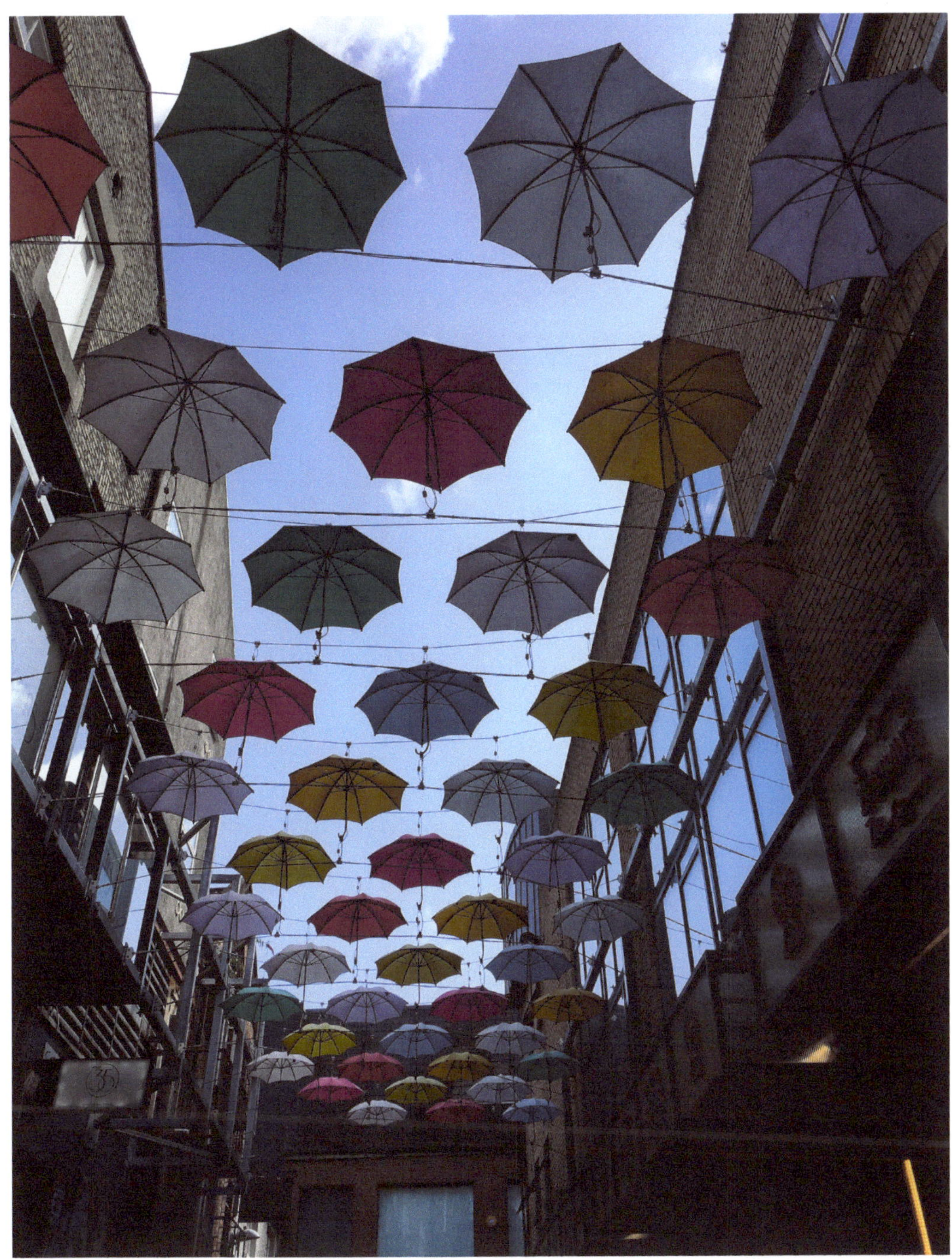

Wonderment: A Moment with…

Viewing sunrise from different perspectives
is wonderment in action as it is expressive.

The laughter of children swinging high in the air,
watch their innocent smiles that they freely share.

The sweet smelling blossoms with colorful petals,
the fragile stems and the breeze that settles.

The waves that crash on a glistening beach,
with intricate sand castles always in reach.

The moon and the tide and the powerful force,
thunder and lightning speak to the source.

Wonderment is felt through
what nature brings.
It is effervescent when
viewed through your own dreams.

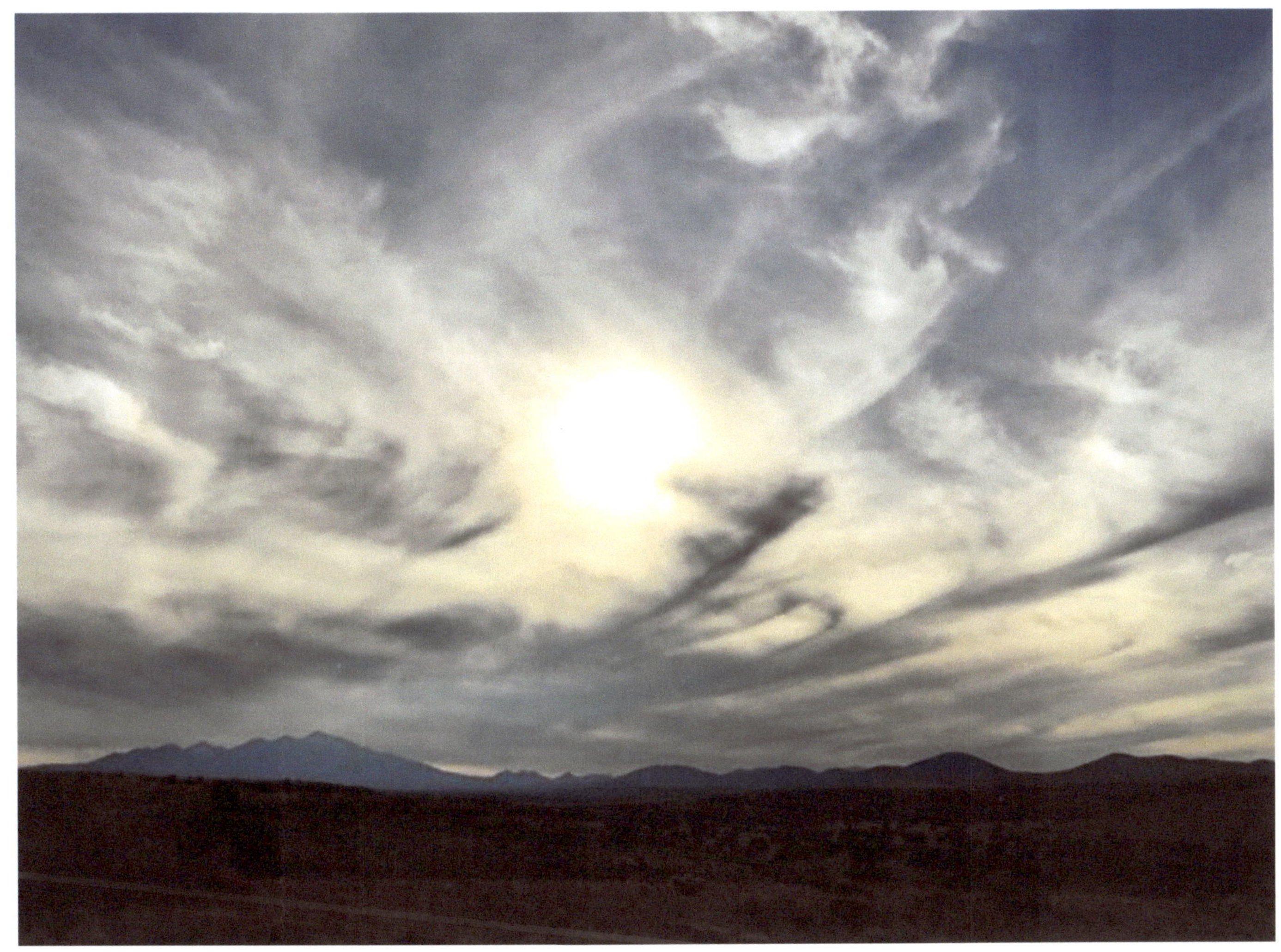

Family and Friendship: A Moment with...

A true friend is one
who lives deep in your heart,
yet never demanding right from the start.

A true friend can always feel your pain
while comforting you with love
and keeping you sane.

True friends are quite close and small in number,
for they will hold you
in times of extreme thunder.

Your best friends support you no matter the cause.
They are your rock "just because."

Nourish your friends with all your soul.
Include your family and cousins
that keep you whole.

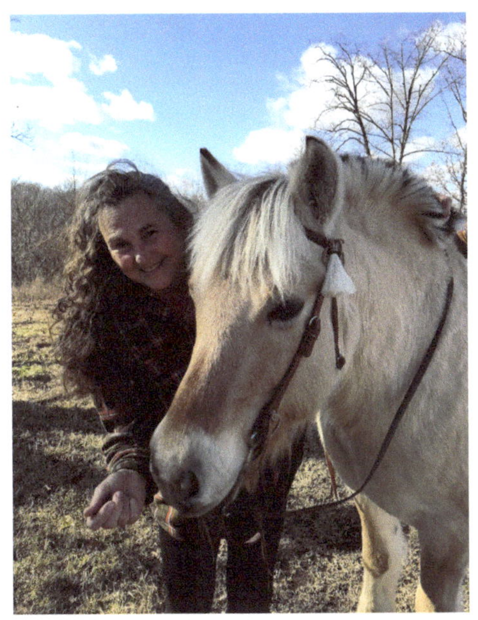

Photographer Catherine Orban

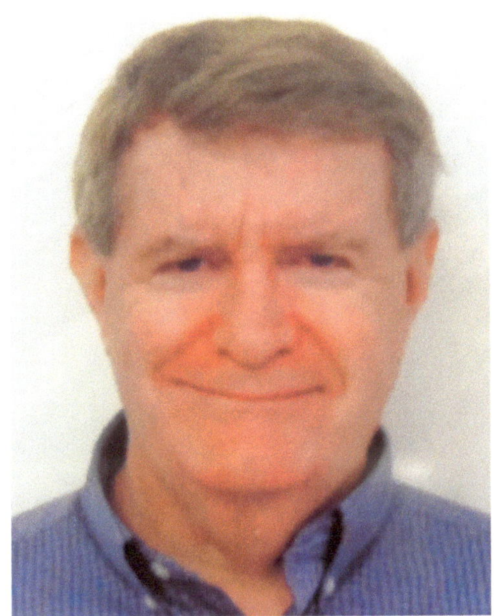

David Gaule

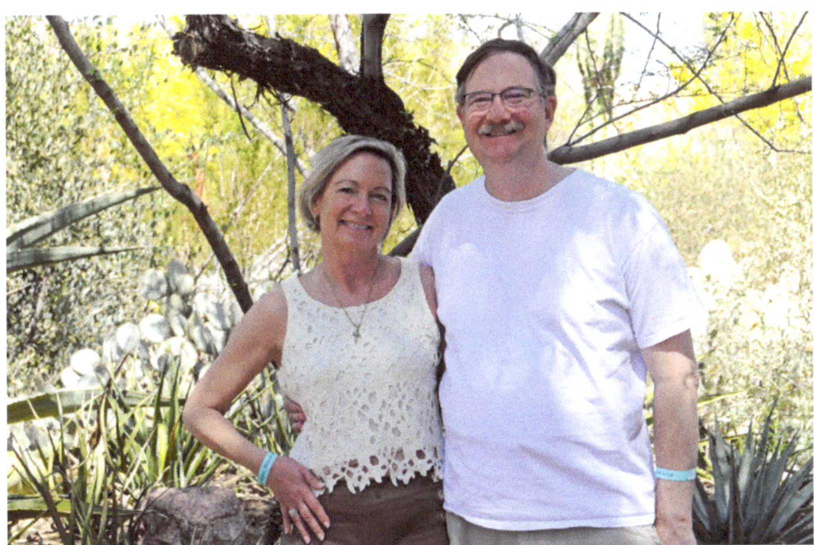

Julianne (author) with her cousin (Photographer) John Grundy

Coming Soon is a short novel that takes place in a small town of Arkansa near the Ozarks. It reads as a true-life story of a female character that reaches insurmountable goals despite devastating circumstances. Her life's goals take her from poor beginnings all the way to stardom. It is a heartwarming love story that will grab your attention of Mama Caves' family.

www.ingramcontent.com/pod-product-compliance
Lightning Source LLC
LaVergne TN
LVHW071629100826
845154LV00007BA/117
9781970153118